# FACTS AT YOUR FINGERTIPS

# INVENTION AND TECHNOLOGY
# AIR AND SPACE

BROWN
BEAR
BOOKS

**Published by Brown Bear Books Ltd**

4877 N. Circulo Bujia
Tucson, AZ 85718
USA

and

First Floor
9-17 St. Albans Place
London N1 0NX

© 2012 Brown Bear Books Ltd

Library of Congress Cataloging-in-Publication Data

Jackson, Tom, 1972-
    Air and space.
           p. cm. – (Facts at your fingertips.
                     Invention and technology)
    Includes index.
    ISBN 978-1-936333-40-0 (library binding)
1.  Aeronautics–Juvenile literature. 2.   Outer space–Exploration-
-Juvenile literature.   I. Title.

TL547.J296 2013
629.1–dc23

2011046995

**Picture Credits**

**Front cover:** Istock
**Back cover:** Shutterstock: Susan Fox

**Alamy**: Interfoto 23; RIA Novosti 51t; **CORBIS**: Roger Ressmeyer 59b; **ESA**: 3; **NASA**: apod 57t; DFRC 28; Earth 40t; GRIN 26t, 36, 42l, 42r, 44l, 51b; History 26b; HSF 48; Images 50, 55t; JPL 52, 57t, 58l; KSC 44r; Langley Research Center 54; NSSCD 53, 59t; Public Domain: 5, 6, 24br, 25t, 29 inset; NASA 55b, 56t, 61b, Towpilot 21; **Shutterstock**: 1, 13bl; Graham Bloomfield 32br, Steve Bower 4; Broukoid 52; Ivan Cholakov 32cl; Margo Harrison 29; ibird 37; T.H. Klimmeck 31; Charles McCarthy 32tl; Bas Rabeling 35; Dario Sabljak 46b; Jennifer Scheer 46t; Martin Smeets 22; John R Smith 30, 60b; Michael Ransburg 19; **Thinkstock**: AbleStock 15; Hemera 40b, 43; istockphoto 12, 18b, 20, 61t; Photos.com 7, 13tr, 14t, 16, 18t, 60t; **Topfoto**: Roger-Viollet 24r; The Granger Collection 25b; ullsteinbild 8, 10; **US Department of Defence**: 34 & B, 49; **Virgin Galactic**: 49.

*Brown Bear Books Ltd has made every attempt to contact the copyright holder. If you have any information please email smortimer@windmillbooks.co.uk*

All artwork copyright Brown Bear Books Ltd

**Editorial Director:** Lindsey Lowe
**Editor:** Tom Jackson
**Creative Director:** Jeni Child
**Designer:** Lynne Lennon
**Children's Publisher:** Anne O'Daly
**Production Director:** Alastair Gourlay

Printed in the United States of America

# CONTENTS

# FLYING WITHOUT WINGS

For centuries people have looked skyward, casting an envious eye at the birds and dreaming of a day when they too could fly.

**The first attempts** at flight used craft that could fly because they were lighter than the air itself—hot-air balloons, for example. Powered flight of heavier-than-air craft came much later.

Before that could happen, however, advances needed to be made in understanding the nature of gases, including the air. Through the work of such pioneers as Anglo-Irish chemist Robert Boyle (1627–1691) people came to

▼ *Hot-air balloons are difficult to steer, and they move wherever the wind takes them. However, many people take a flight in a hot-air balloon to enjoy the spectacular views.*

## THE FIRST BALLOONISTS?

Between 500 B.C. and A.D. 900, the people of the Nazca culture drew huge figures on the desert plains, near the coast of Peru in South America. Many of these gigantic pictures of animals are only visible from the air. Some scientists believe that this ancient culture knew how to fly in balloons to view the images. Nazca potters often decorated their pots with pictures of balloons and kites, and Nazca textiles show pictures of flying men. In the 1970s Nazca fabrics were tested by a modern balloon-making company. The company found that the traditional fabrics had a tighter weave than the material the company made themselves, making them ideal for hot-air ballooning. In 1975 the International Explorers Society of Miami made their own balloon, *Condor I*, based on Peruvian designs and materials. The balloon was filled with hot smoke produced by burning dry wood. Scorched circles of rock found near the giant artworks might have been created by similar fires centuries ago. *Condor I* rose 380 ft (116 m) into the air and descended safely after several minutes. This does not prove that the ancient Peruvians knew how to fly but shows that it was a possibility.

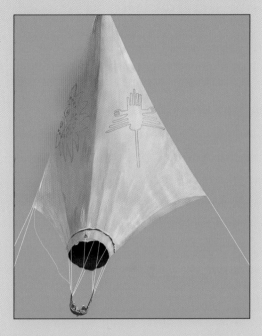

▲ *A two-man crew tested* Condor I, *sitting on a cradle made from bundles of reeds.*

realize that different gases had different weights, and that the gas contained in a "bubble" would rise if it was lighter than the gas outside the bubble.

### The Montgolfier brothers

On a sunny June day in 1783, French brothers Joseph-Michel Montgolfier (1740–1810) and Jacques-Étienne Montgolfier (1745–1799) unveiled their new invention in the marketplace in Annonay, southern France. The brothers burned straw and wood under a specially designed bag and thrilled onlookers, who watched open mouthed as the Western world's first hot-air balloon soared 3,000 ft (910 m) into

## BALLOONS IN EAST ASIA

More than 2,000 years ago, Chinese children played a game that created tiny hot-air balloons. Historical records explain that children placed a few dry twigs inside empty eggshells and then set the twigs alight to send the eggshells flying. Centuries later, in the 1200s, the Mongol people from the wide open plains of Central Asia would launch a dragon-shaped hot-air balloon to mark rallying points. The first ascent of a hot-air balloon in the Western world, however, did not occur until about 500 years later.

the air. A few months later they repeated the display in front of the French king and queen, only this time they also sent a few farm animals in a basket under the balloon. A few months later balloons were carrying humans high into the air for the first time.

**The birth of the airship**

It was not possible to steer the earliest hot-air balloons. There was no power source small enough and light enough to fit in a balloon's basket. Balloons were at the mercy of the winds, unless they were tethered to the ground.

The advantages that could be gained by having a free-floating, controllable balloon were

▲ *The flight of the Montgolfier brothers' first balloon in Annonay, France, was watched by a large audience.*

obvious. As the 19th century came to a close, every military power that could afford such a program was rushing to build a "ship of the air." Considering the pioneering efforts of the French, it is not surprising that a Frenchman, Henri Giffard (1825–1882), was the first person to create such an aircraft.

As early as 1852, Giffard designed and built the world's first "dirigible" (from the French

## THE FIRST HUMAN FLIGHT

The Montgolfiers' 1783 demonstration in Versailles sent a sheep, a duck, and a chicken into the air. (The animals returned safely but failed to make it beyond Christmas dinner.) It was watched by Marquis d'Arlandes (1742–1809) and his good friend François Pilâtre de Rozier (1757–1785) who then set about becoming the first people to take to the skies in a free-floating hot-air balloon. On a crisp, clear November day in 1783, the two men ascended into the skies over Paris in a Montgolfier balloon. Their 5.5 mile (9 km) journey above the city caused an uproar at the time. When the balloon eventually landed in a field on the outskirts of Paris, a group of peasant workers dropped to their knees in prayer, believing the two adventurers to be angels sent by God.

## PUTTING BALLOONS TO WORK

While balloons provided entertaining diversions from the routine of 18th-century life, they appeared at first to have no practical use. One man, however, soon realized that he could use tethered balloons to his advantage. French general Napoleon Bonaparte (1769–1821), who later became the emperor of France, formed the world's first ever military airborne division. Known as the Aérostiers, this intrepid group of tethered balloonists gave the French Army an advantage by revealing the exact location of an enemy's troops. For much of the following hundred years tethered balloons were used in this capacity by many armies, including both sides during the American Civil War (1861–1865).

▲ *A hydrogen balloon, known as* Intrepid, *is inflated by a surveillance unit during the American Civil War. A spotter aboard the balloon gave reports on the movements of the enemy force.*

*diriger*, meaning "to steer"). Rather than use a normal balloon-shaped bag, Giffard used an elongated cigar-shaped bag full of hydrogen. His ship was powered by a steam engine weighing 350 lb (150 kg), so Giffard had to use a gas bag 144 ft (44 m) long. He started out from Paris on his first flight and traveled 17 miles (27 km), reaching a top speed of 6 mph (10 km/h).

Unfortunately for Giffard, however, his craft was fated always to be underpowered. Although his dirigible was a significant improvement on the ordinary balloon, any aircraft possessing a top speed of 6 mph was always going to be uncontrollable in wind speeds of 7 mph (11 km/h) or more. This situation improved in 1872 when German engineer Paul Haenlein fitted the recently invented (and considerably lighter)

internal-combustion engine to a dirigible. To save weight, Haenlein used the super-light hydrogen gas in the balloon as fuel, although this did reduce the distance the craft could travel before it began to lose height. In 1883

### WORDS TO KNOW

- **Atom:** The smallest units in a substance.
- **Dense:** A description of how much mass is packed into a substance.
- **Hydrogen:** A highly flammable gas that is lighter than air.
- **Internal-combustion:** The engine system used in cars and trucks.

French brothers Albert Tissandier and Gaston Tissandier became the first people to power a dirigible with an electric motor.

## Zeppelins

The greatest dirigible designer was Count Ferdinand von Zeppelin (1838–1917). Zeppelin had been a cavalryman in the Prussian (German) army and a volunteer for the Union Army in the American Civil War. While in the United States he flew in hot-air balloons and devoted the rest of his life to building bigger and better flying machines. Zeppelin added a lightweight frame to the gas bag, making it more rigid, so that the dirigible would remain controllable at the higher speeds.

On July 2, 1900, Zeppelin took his early "airship" on its first flight, over Lake Constance

▲ The Graf Zeppelin (LZ-127) made 590 flights between 1928 and 1937 and traveled more than a million miles in its lifetime. It was broken up in 1940.

in Germany. The flight lasted just 17 minutes before *Luftschiff Zeppelin One (LZ-1)*, dropped to the surface of the lake. It was to be another eight years before Zeppelin's first truly successful flight, with *LZ-4*. At the time *LZ-4* was the largest airship in the skies. It was an incredible 446 ft (136 m) long and required 500,000 cubic ft (14,000 m³) of hydrogen to get off the ground. On July 4, 1908, *LZ-4* traveled at a continuous 40 mph (60 km/h) for 12 hours over Switzerland. At last, practical, powered, controllable air travel had arrived.

Between 1910 and the outbreak of World War I in 1914 about 34,000 people had their first taste of air travel in a Zeppelin airship. The war spurred on airship construction, and Germany led the world in airship design and construction at this time, building 88 military

---

## THE HYDROGEN BALLOON

Hot air was not the only thing being used to inflate balloons in 1783. The French physicist Jacques-Alexandre Charles (1746–1823) took to the air with fellow Frenchman Nicolas Robert just six months after the Montgolfier brothers first demonstrated their hot-air balloon. Using a balloon that had been filled with hydrogen (the lightest of all gases), the two men must have wondered what they had let themselves in for when their craft shot nearly one mile (1.6 km) up into the sky. Charles and Robert eventually returned safely to the ground, and despite their early scare made many more flights.

## SOCIETY AND INVENTIONS

### Why balloons and airships fly

To fly, airships and balloons need to generate enough lift to counteract gravity, which is constantly pulling them back to Earth. The Montgolfier brothers knew that hot air rises and they realized that they could make a balloon go up as well by filling it with hot gas. When they heated ordinary air, the minute gas particles (made of atoms) began to move around faster and spread out. This made the air inside the balloon less dense than the cold air around it. The balloon was therefore lighter than the surrounding air, and so it floated upward. When the air cooled, the balloon returned to the ground again. Jacques-Alexandre Charles was also aware of the principles of lighter-than-air flight. He reasoned, however, that it should be possible to take to the skies by filling a balloon with a gas that was naturally less dense than air at normal temperatures. Gases such as helium or hydrogen, for example, are made up of particles that are much smaller and lighter than those of the oxygen and nitrogen gases that make up the air.

A Light particles inside airship
B Hot particles inside gas balloon
C Cold air particles

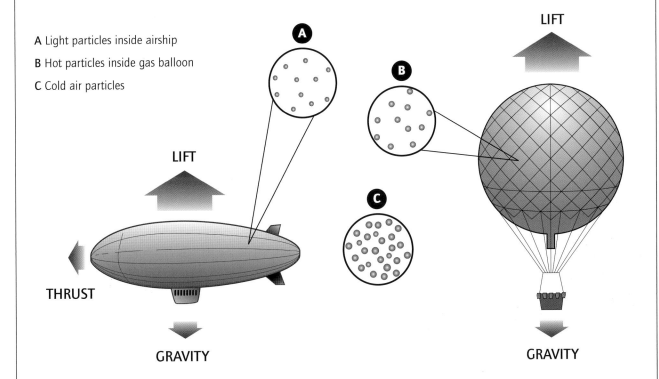

▲ When the lift force acting on the balloon or airship is bigger than the force of gravity, then the aircraft will move upward.

The airship's engine also creates another force—thrust—that pushes the machine forward through the air.

airships. London, England, had the dubious honor of being the first city to be attacked from the air when a group of "zeppelins" made a raid.

## The demise of the airship

Between 1920 and 1933 the U.S. Navy built five airships. Three of them crashed: the *Shenandoah* (1925), the *Akron* (1933), and the *Macon* (1935). In 1936, Germany's *Hindenburg* began regular transatlantic crossings. Unfortunately for all concerned, this proved to be the final chapter in the history of the airship. Although hydrogen is the lightest of all gases, it is also one of the most flammable. The *Hindenburg* crashed tragically the following year, and never again would airships of this magnitude be built.

▼ *The zeppelin* Hindenburg *exploded while docking at the Lakehurst Air Station in New Jersey in 1937. The disaster was probably caused by a spark of static electricity that set the hydrogen bags inside alight.*

### AIRSHIPS AS AIRLINERS

In the 1920s there were few planes that could offer the same long-distance travel opportunities as airships. Large airships, such as the British *R101*, were equipped to carry passengers over long distances, carried in gondolas positioned below the main gas bags. Airships had to be light so that the amount of gas needed to lift them was kept to a minimum. Therefore, they were made of light materials, such as aluminum. Travelers could view the world below from promenades, which were closed in with windows made of lightweight plastic alternatives to glass. Unfortunately, in October 1930, the *R101* crashed in France on its first flight, killing all but 6 of the 54 people on board. Similar fatal crashes made it clear that hydrogen airships were just too dangerous.

### Balloons and airships today

Hot-air balloons are now mostly used for leisure activities. Scientists use hydrogen gas balloons to carry equipment very high into the sky to study the upper atmosphere and monitor weather conditions. The airship is no longer used for transportation. Modern airships are filled with helium gas, which is slightly heavier than hydrogen but much safer. Helium blimps are often used for flying adverts at sports games and other large public events.

## KEY COMPONENTS

### Inside airships

Nonrigid airships (or blimps) have no internal framework to support the shape of the outer envelope, which is filled with gas and one or more air-filled ballonets. Air can be released from the ballonets or pumped in to increase or decrease lift. Rigid airships (or zeppelins) have an internal framework that supports the outer envelope.

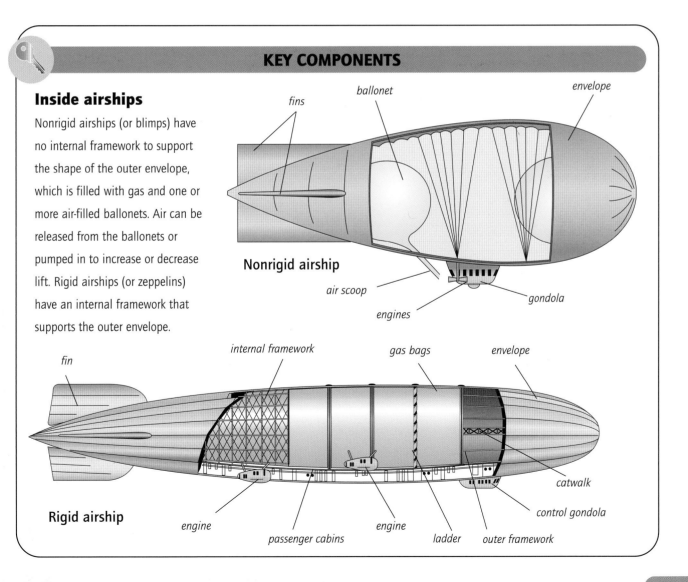

Nonrigid airship

fins
ballonet
envelope
air scoop
engines
gondola

Rigid airship

fin
internal framework
gas bags
envelope
engine
passenger cabins
engine
ladder
outer framework
control gondola
catwalk

# THE AGE OF PROPELLERS

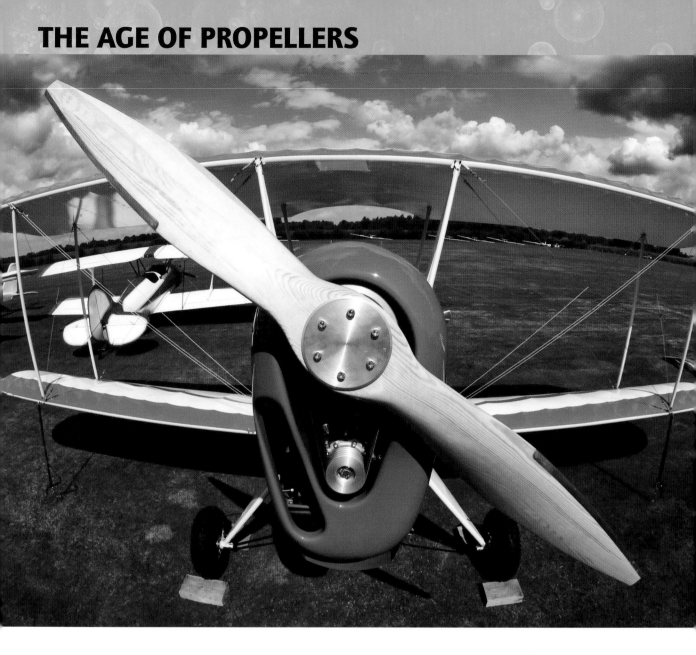

It took another 120 years of invention after the first balloonists floated into the air for winged aircraft to finally swoop into the sky.

**Hot-air balloons** and gas-filled airships only fly because they are lighter than air. Balloons are at the mercy of the wind, and while airships could be steered, they were slow and very dangerous. People could still only dream of flying in safe, fast, controllable craft. However, long before the

▲ The first fixed-wing aircraft were powered by propeller engines. A spinning propeller's shape pushes air backward—and the airplane forward—in much the same way as a ship's propeller moves it through water.

last of the great hydrogen-filled airships had come to a terrible and fiery end, the skies were buzzing with a new sound.

### Early pioneers
Before the invention of hot-air and gas balloons, it had been assumed that if humans were to fly,

it would be by imitating the birds. Would-be aeronautical engineers designed impractical aircraft fitted with flapping wings. In 1680, however, Italian scientist Giovanni A. Borelli (1608–1679) proved that people's chest muscles are not big enough to flap the large wings that would be needed to lift them into the air.

It was not until 1804 that the first working model of an aircraft with fixed wings was made, by British scientist Sir George Cayley (1773–1857). Cayley's glider also had a rigid body (or fuselage) and a tail with a rudder and moveable control surfaces that could be used to send the craft up or down. He had established

## ICARUS

An ancient Greek legend tells about an inventor named Daedalus and his son Icarus, who flew using wings made of wax and feathers. Icarus did not know the limits of the invention and flew too high and close to the Sun. The wax melted and Icarus fell to his death.

▲ *Daedalus looks down on the body of his son in this 18th-century drawing of the Icarus legend.*

## LEONARDO DA VINCI

The great Italian artist and scientist Leonardo da Vinci (1452–1519) dreamed of taking to the air in all manner of devices. His drawings included plans for an airplane, a simple parachute, and this sail-powered helicopter.

▲ *Da Vinci imagined his helicopter's screw-shaped sail would pull the craft into the air when it was spun around.*

the basic structure of modern airplanes. Cayley spent the next 50 years testing his ideas before building a full-sized glider. Finally, in 1853, Cayley's coachman took to the air in the first ever successful flight of a full-sized glider and the first successful use of the curved "airfoil" wing shape. All Cayley's glider needed to become a plane was an engine and propeller. Unfortunately, those engines that existed at the time were too heavy, large, and inefficient.

Many others contributed to the development of gliders, such as the American Octave Chanute

and the German Otto Lillienthal (1848–1896), who recorded his research in a book, *The Flight of Birds as the Basis of Flying*.

## The Wright brothers

The work of Lillienthal and Chanute inspired two brothers in Dayton, Ohio. Having studied the work of Cayley and Lillienthal, bicyclemakers and printers Wilbur Wright (1867–1912) and Orville Wright (1871–1948) set about designing

▶ *German aviator Otto Lillienthal built gliders with curved wings to create lift. Some of the gliders were large enough to carry him, and Lillienthal died in a crash in 1896.*

## SCIENTIFIC PRINCIPLES

## Airfoil shapes and lift forces

Swiss academic Daniel Bernoulli (1700–1782) proved that the pressure of a fluid (gas or liquid) decreases as its speed increases. This discovery was to have a far-reaching effect on the design of airplane wings. Being well aware of the work of Bernoulli, Sir George Cayley investigated how air passing over a wing affects the amount of lift a wing generates. Bernoulli's theory indicated that if the speed of air passing over the wing was greater than that of the air passing under the wing, a pressure difference would occur that, if great enough, would cause the wing to lift upward. That force would raise it—and any craft to which it was attached—into the air. Cayley's work laid the foundation of aerodynamics (which includes the scientific principles of flight) and led to the development of the airfoil shape of an airplane's wings.

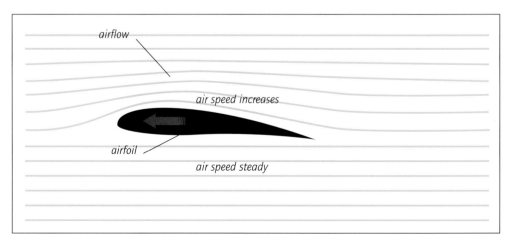

## KITES: THE FIRST WINGED AIRCRAFT

▲ *Kites fly using the same principles as fixed-winged aircraft.*

The first heavier-than-air craft to be flown were probably kites. The ancient Chinese discovered how to make kites between 400 and 300 B.C. A few hundred years later the Chinese authorities were strapping serious offenders to enormous kites and sending them aloft, screaming in terror. More than 2,000 years later Lawrence Hargrave (1850–1915), an Australian draftsman, began to experiment with kites. In 1894 he was lifted 16 ft (5 m) off the ground by four box kites of his own making. Some people have claimed that Hargrave's work had little impact on the history of flight since he was working in Australia, cut off from the mainstream of aviation history in the United States and Europe. However, many of Hargrave's ideas were used in early aircraft: the wings of many early planes resembled box kites, for example. Like other early aviators, Hargrave also confirmed that wings with curved surfaces (airfoil shapes) flew better than flat wings.

controllable gliders. From watching buzzards in flight, the brothers knew that a successful aircraft would have to be able to bank to one side or another, climb or descend, and turn from left to right. The last glider the Wrights built, in 1902, could perform all these movements. They had also built a wind tunnel to test that the glider's wing and surface shapes were aerodynamic. Now all that remained was to add a lightweight engine and propeller so it could power its own takeoff, flight, and landing.

Previous engineers had tried to power their planes with heavy steam engines; the Wright brothers were lucky enough to be able to make use of the recently invented internal-combustion engine. The brothers designed and built a small gasoline engine and connected it to a pair of propellers (also designed by the brothers) with bicycle chains. Their glider was now an airplane.

On December 17, 1903, Orville Wright took off from level ground in the first powered airplane—Flyer I (popularly known as Kitty Hawk). The Wright brothers continued to experiment with airplanes throughout 1904, making a number of improvements in the way the original aircraft handled. In 1905 they built Flyer III—the world's first practical airplane. It could turn, bank, circle, fly figures of eight, and remain airborne for more than half an hour. The Wright brothers then refused to fly again until they got financial backing from the government or a private company.

At last, in 1908 the U.S. government issued a contract to the Wright brothers for an airplane that could carry a pilot and an observer for 125 miles (200 km). The two brothers delivered just such an aircraft one year later. Their plane was a remarkable improvement in the technology that just six years earlier was capable only of carrying a single aviator for 170 ft (51.5 m). Within a year every major army in the world had been equipped with a force of airplanes.

## The effect of war

It is one of the unfortunate truths of history that technology always takes massive leaps forward

▼ The Wright brothers' Flyer 1 was different to modern planes in several ways. It had elevators at the front instead of on the tail. The steering system used wires to bend the wings to alter the way lift acted on the aircraft.

during wartime because new weapons can tip the balance from defeat to victory. Although originally conceived as a means of spying on the enemy, military airplanes were soon fitted with weapons. October 30, 1911, marks the day when modern air war began. An Italian pilot on a

rudder

propeller

runner

elevators

## SCIENTIFIC PRINCIPLES

### Forces acting on a plane

To be able to fly, an airplane has to generate enough lift and thrust to overcome gravity, which is constantly pulling the plane back toward Earth, and drag (the resistance of the air to objects passing through it). The airfoil (curved) shape of an airplane's wing enables it to generate lift; thrust is generated by the airplane's engine and, if it has them, propellers, which act like airfoils. For a glider to fly, it has to be towed until it reaches a speed at which its wings are generating enough lift to fly. The pilots of the first gliders had to run down slopes and use the wind to take off.

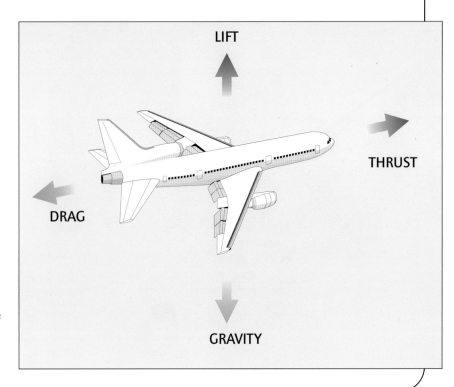

spying mission over Libya during a war between Italy and Turkey took it upon himself to drop four hand grenades onto the enemy trenches below, thereby changing forever the way war would, in future, be waged. By the time World War I (1914–1918) broke out in Europe, all sides were equipped with warplanes.

### Biplanes

The stresses placed on an airplane during combat are far greater than those experienced during normal passenger flights. The greatest problem facing aircraft manufacturers at that time was how to design airplanes that were both lightweight and strong. Several designs, using between one and four sets of wings, were tested, but the design that best met the requirements of lightness and strength was that of the biplane.

The biplane design stacks one wing on top of another to create a boxlike structure. The real beauty of the biplane design was the way struts and bracing wires were cleverly arranged to take advantage of the inbuilt strength of triangular-based structures. By running bracing wires diagonally from the base of a strut on the lower wing to the top of a strut on the upper wing, it was possible to create a structure so rigid that it would collapse only on impact with something solid (usually the ground). The only drawback of

◀ *A biplane's super-strong wings make it ideal for performing spectacular acrobatic maneuvers that would cripple faster but less tough aircraft.*

## FLYING BOATS

Seaplanes are aircraft that can land and take off from water. Instead of wheels—or in many cases, as well as—the undercarriage is equipped with large floats. The first seaplane was built by Henri Fabre (1882–1984) in France in 1910. A flying boat is a type of seaplane that is supported on the water by its main body, which is hull-shaped, like a boat. The first flying boat was invented by U.S. aviation pioneer Glenn Curtiss in 1912. In the 1930s flying boats were often used for intercontinental travel: there was a shortage of airports outside North America and Europe, so flying boats were ideal since they did not need airports. By the 1950s, however, flying boats had largely been replaced by land-based aircraft. Until the arrival of helicopters, flying boats were also used in air–sea rescues.

the biplane was that the twin wings, bracing wires, and struts caused a great deal of drag, slowing the plane down and increasing fuel consumption. Nevertheless, biplanes pushed back the boundaries of aviation. In 1919, two British pilots flew across the Atlantic Ocean in a large Vickers biplane, taking under 17 hours to fly from Newfoundland to Ireland.

### Monoplanes

As new ultrastrong yet lightweight materials were being created, it became possible to design airplanes with single wings—called monoplanes.

The first practical monoplane was actually built as early as 1907 by French engineer Louis

▲ *Flying boats are ideal transportation in rugged mountain regions, where there are few runways—or even roads—but plenty of large lakes to land on.*

Blériot (1872-1936), who flew an improved version of this plane across the English Channel two years later. In 1927, U.S. airmail pilot Charles Lindbergh (1902-1974), now one of the best-known figures in aviation history, made the first nonstop solo flight across the Atlantic in the Spirit of St. Louis, a monoplane. The monoplane design was not widely adopted, however, until World War II (1939-1945).

Since WWII virtually every plane built has been a monoplane. Another major advance

## WORDS TO KNOW

- **Airfoil:** The curved shape of a wing which is needed to create a lift force.
- **Aviator:** A person who flies aircraft.
- **Fuselage:** The body of an airplane, containing the cockpit and passenger cabin.
- **Wingspan:** The distance from one wing tip to the other.

## KEY COMPONENTS

### Light planes

Modern light planes vary little from the design of early monoplanes. Most have a single engine, driving a propeller, and can seat from one to ten people. However, instead of being built from wood and fabric, today's light aircraft are made from metals or strong plastics. They seldom weigh more than 12,000 pounds (5,500 kg). The basic parts of a light plane are the wings, fuselage (body), tail assembly, and landing gear. Light planes, such as Cessnas and Pipers, are a widely used form of transportation in the United States and sparsely populated countries, such as Canada and Australia.

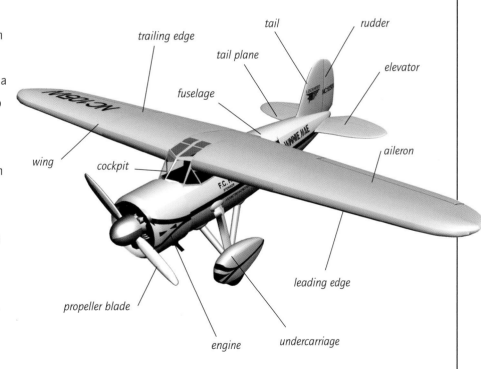

▲ The wings and tail planes have an airfoil shape. The pilot steers using moveable flaps on the back—or trailing—edges, which direct the air flowing over the plane.

▲ *The Messerschmitt 109, otherwise known as an Me-109, was the main high-speed fighter used by the German air force in World War II.*

was made in materials. The earliest planes were made of wood and fabric; the 1920s saw fabric-covered metal-framed planes; WWII saw the introduction of all-metal planes.

During WWII it soon became clear that no side could win a battle unless it had control of the air, and it was to be the fighter aircraft that would decide who took control. The first battle to be fought entirely in the air was the Battle of Britain, during which the Germans bombed southern Britain in 1940 in what was to prove to be an unsuccessful invasion attempt.

## FACTS AND FIGURES

● The 1927 Lockheed Vega, a monoplane, had a wingspan of 41 ft (12.5 m) and a 425-horsepower (318 kilowatt) engine.

● The Hughes H-4 Hercules flying boat, or "Spruce Goose", had a wingspan of 321 ft (97.5 m), the largest of any aircraft. Built in 1947, the giant wooden plane flew only once, covering approximately 1 mile (1.6 km).

The battle for air control was as much a battle between opposing designs as it was between opposite sides in the war: Supermarine Aviation's Spitfire and the Hawker (later British

Aerospace) company's Hurricane were pitted against the less romantically named Me-109 made by German company Messerschmitt. When the United States and Japan entered the war at the end of 1941, it was the Japanese company Mitsubishi that supplied the remarkable A6M. Known to the Allies as the Zero, this fighter made the best of a small engine by being the strongest and lightest fighter in the war. Initially it outclassed any U.S. fighter it came up against, but soon met its match in the United States' Grumman F6F Hellcat and P-51 Mustang.

By the end of the war, the propeller-driven airplane had reached the limit of its design capabilities. If airplanes were to get any faster, they would need a new kind of engine.

## SOCIETY AND INVENTIONS

### The first modern airliners

In 1933, the U.S. company Boeing designed the Boeing 247. Previous airliners (passenger- or freight-carrying planes) were very limited in how far they could fly and how many people they could carry. The Boeing 247 marked a revolution in airliner design. Fast, with a cruising speed of 180 mph (300 km/h), it could travel for up to 750 miles (1,200 km) before it had to stop for more fuel. Two years later, the Douglas Aircraft Company launched the DC-3, which could out fly the 247 and cover 1,000 miles (1,600 km) in less than 5 hours. The DC-3, or Dakota, as it is also known, was the main airliner until the 1950s.

▲ More than 16,000 DC-3s were built for use as airliners and cargo planes. Around 400 are still airworthy today. The plane was considerably wider than earlier passenger aircraft, so up to 32 passengers could be carried, sitting in rows of four seats.

# THE JET AGE AND BEYOND

The invention of the jet engine brought about a revolution in flight. Jet-propelled aircraft were powerful enough to move faster than sound itself, fly to the very edge of space, and even to hover in midair.

**As the roaring** 1920s reached their climax, a few pioneering airplane designers had begun to realize that there was nowhere left for them to go. A greater understanding of how objects move through the air—the science of aerodynamics—had inevitably led to sleeker, faster aircraft that could cut through the sky without being damaged. However, it was beginning to become apparent that the normal arrangement of engine and propeller was an inadequate power source for the future requirements of modern aviation.

## PROPELLER SPEED LIMITS

As faster and more powerful aircraft were developed, air, the very medium through which their creations traveled, became the enemy of the airplane designer. Up until this point the air passing over the surfaces of an airplane had behaved like a fluid, flowing around the craft and reacting to provide the necessary lift to keep it off the ground. But some engineers had realized that at speeds approaching 700 mph (1,100 km/h), the air behaves differently. Drag (air resistance) on the airplane increases to the point at which the air forms shock waves that buffet the aircraft body. This reduces lift so much that the pilot loses control. An airplane's propellers always move faster than the rest of the craft and so will be the first part of the airplane to suffer from this problem. In effect, the behavior of the air around the propeller imposes a strict limit on the speeds that can be reached by aircraft powered in this way. A new type of engine was needed if higher speeds were to be reached.

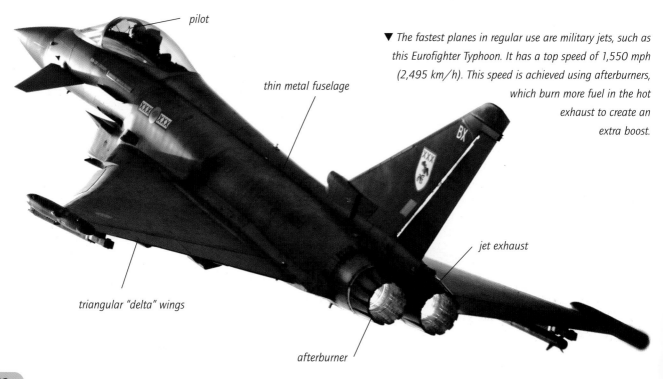

pilot

thin metal fuselage

▼ The fastest planes in regular use are military jets, such as this Eurofighter Typhoon. It has a top speed of 1,550 mph (2,495 km/h). This speed is achieved using afterburners, which burn more fuel in the hot exhaust to create an extra boost.

jet exhaust

triangular "delta" wings

afterburner

**New engines**

The military's continual need for faster aircraft encouraged the development of new engines. In the 1930s, scientists in both the United States and Germany were investigating the possibility of using rockets as airplane engines. The German researchers were led by Wernher von Braun (1912–1977) and the Americans by Robert Hutchings Goddard (1882–1945). However, rocket engines proved to be very expensive to fuel. They were also very hard to control and frequently exploded.

---

## ROCKET PLANES

Before the jet engine was widely adopted, scientists experimented with using rocket engines to make planes travel faster. In Germany as early as 1928 Alexander M. Lippisch (1894–1976) had designed the world's first successful rocket plane. It was a tailless glider fitted with two rocket engines that used a solid fuel source. The first operational liquid-fuel rocket plane, the Messerschmitt Me-163 Komet (below), drew heavily on Lippisch's design. The Komet could reach speeds of more than 600 mph (970 km/h), but it could not fly for long and often exploded on landing. Military aircraft manufacturers have since occasionally built rocket planes, mostly to carry out research on traveling at high speeds and high altitudes. The Bell X-1, for example, was the first plane to fly faster than the speed of sound. The United States' *X-15* rocket plane flew over 310,000 ft (over 95,000 m, or 95 km) above Earth in 1962 and later traveled at five times the speed of sound.

Meanwhile, in Britain engineer Frank Whittle patented the jet engine in 1930. He then joined forces with a handful of friends and formed a company called Power Jets, Ltd. By 1937 Whittle and his associates had built an operational jet engine in their workshop. The jet age had finally arrived. It was not until the 1950s, though, that the jet engine came into widespread use; people were unaware until then that as well as making planes go faster, jet engines could sharply reduce the cost of air travel.

Whittle's invention used a jet of hot gases to push the aircraft along. The stream of gases was produced by drawing air into the engine using a fanlike turbine. The air was then used to burn some fuel inside a central combustion chamber, producing the blast of hot exhaust gases that created the thrust.

### The first jet-powered airplane

The British government was reluctant to fund Whittle's research. They threw away the opportunity to be the first military power to build a jet-powered airplane, and the honor went instead to the German-based company Heinkel. Working independently of Frank Whittle, three German engineers—Hans von Ohain, Herbert Wagner, and Helmut Schelp—had investigated the idea of the jet engine. On August 27, 1939, the Heinkel He-178, powered

---

## THE FIRST JET AIRCRAFT?

In 1910, a Romanian inventor named Henri Coanda (1886–1972) built an aircraft that was pushed along by a jet of gas. However, it worked in a different way to modern jet engines, and so few people recognize Coanda as the inventor of jet aircraft (though in 2010 Romanians celebrated 100 years of jet travel in their countryman's honor). Coanda's jet used a piston engine to spin a fan inside, which drew air in the front and pushed it out the back, creating thrust. The *Coanda-1910* aircraft never flew. It caught fire on the runway during its first takeoff. However, Coanda's "motor-jet" was used in other ways, powering a sled built for Grand Duke Cyril of Russia. Coanda is better remembered for describing the Coanda Effect, in which liquids are attracted to nearby solid surfaces.

▲ *The motor-jet propulsion system was positioned at the front of the* Coanda-1910 *biplane.*

▶ *Grand Duke Cyril in his unique jet-powered motor sledge in 1910.*

◄ *An Me-262, one of the few makes of jet aircraft to fly in WWII, is hidden away in a forest airbase during the last few weeks of the war.*

by a jet engine designed by von Ohain, took to the skies over Germany.

It took the outbreak of World War II (1939–1945) to get the British government to take Whittle's ideas seriously, giving the Germans a two-year head start in jet-engine technology. The British government eventually took over Power Jets, Ltd, in 1944, just in time to see the Gloster Meteor, the Royal Air Force's first operational jet fighter, go into battle against enemy Messerschmitt's Me-262.

By the time WWII ended in 1945, it was clear to all sides that military combat planes were going to have to be jet powered for future conflicts. But with the economies of so many European countries now in tatters, it was left to the United States to lead the way in developing aircraft-engine technology.

The early jet designs were far from perfect, and there were, of course, many variations on Whittle's relatively simple design. One of the first improvements made to the jet engine was

## FRANK WHITTLE

As early as 1928 a young cadet at the Royal Air Force College in Cranwell, England, put forward the idea of replacing the traditional piston-powered engine with a new power source called a turbojet. The cadet, Frank Whittle (1907–1996), had been quick to realize that there would soon be a demand for an airplane that could fly much faster than any speed achieved using a propeller. In 1928 Whittle, the son of an engineer, submitted plans to the college in which he set out his ideas for a jet-propelled airplane. Unfortunately, Whittle's work was not well received by the British government, which dismissed it out of hand, declaring his vision to be an impractical dream. Whittle, however, was convinced that he was on the right track.

► *Frank Whittle inspects an engine of his design on an early jet fighter.*

the inclusion of an afterburner. In Whittle's original engine less than a third of the air drawn in at the front was actually used to burn fuel in the combustion chamber. The remaining air passed out of the rear of the engine with the rest of the exhaust gases. By injecting more fuel into the hot exhaust gases, it was possible to gain a 40 percent increase in the amount of thrust produced by the engine on takeoff. Once the airplane was in the air and

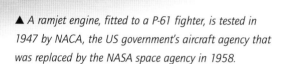

▲ *A ramjet engine, fitted to a P-61 fighter, is tested in 1947 by NACA, the US government's aircraft agency that was replaced by the NASA space agency in 1958.*

## CHUCK YEAGER

Assigned to the U.S. Army Air Corps after enlisting in 1941, Chuck Yeager was an outstanding fighter pilot during WWII, flying 64 missions and shooting down a record-breaking four German fighter planes in a single dogfight. After the war, Yeager served briefly as a flight instructor before taking on the far more challenging role of test pilot. When the Bell company requested a volunteer to act as test pilot for its secret new project, the X-1, Yeager jumped at the chance, even though many fine pilots had already lost their lives trying to break the sound barrier.

traveling at speed, the improvement in thrust was much greater.

**Breaking the sound barrier**

It had long been one of the goals of aviation engineers the world over to smash through the invisible obstacle known as the sound barrier. Nevertheless, smashing through this invisible barrier became the goal of the engineers at the U.S. Bell Aircraft Company. All they needed was a highly sophisticated craft and someone brave enough, skilled enough, and foolhardy enough to fly it. This person was Captain Charles "Chuck" Yeager (born 1923).

The X-1 was an unusual airplane. Essentially a small rocket equipped with four combustion chambers that could be fired independently, it had to be "towed" up into the air strapped underneath a Boeing B-29 bomber. The plan was that at around 30,000 ft (9,100 m) the X-1 would be dropped from the B-29, and Yeager would fire the first of the rocket

## SCIENTIFIC PRINCIPLES

### How a jet engine works

Jet engines draw in air at the front of the engine. This air is then squeezed and put under pressure by a device called a compressor. Then fuel is added to the compressed air and the resulting mixture ignited in a part of the engine called the combustion chamber. The fuel burns into a mixture of gases, releasing a lot of heat—temperatures inside rise to around 700°F (370°C). The heat makes the exhaust gases expand rapidly. This hot, fast-moving exhaust flows out of the back of the engine after first passing through a turbine (which is there to drive fuel pumps, electricity generators, and the compressor at the front of the engine). Jet engines are placed under the wings of the airplane or inside the rear part of the main body (fuselage), with the exhaust gases exiting from beneath the tail.

The way a jet engine works had been described centuries before, in an age when few people traveled faster than a horse could carry them. In the 17th century, the English physicist Isaac Newton (1642–1727) drew up three laws of motion. The third law states that for every action there is an equal and opposite reaction. This means that when hot exhaust gases are ejected at tremendous speeds from the rear of a jet engine, a resulting opposite force drives the engine—and anything attached to it—forward.

### Turbofan

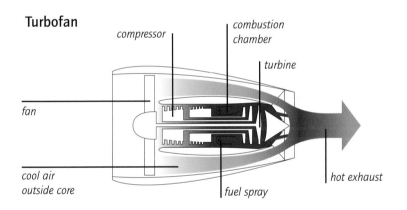

*compressor*
*combustion chamber*
*turbine*
*fan*
*cool air outside core*
*fuel spray*
*hot exhaust*

◄ *Airliners use turbofan engines. They have a large propeller-like fan, at the front, which draws air into the compresser and also pushes cold air around the engine core, creating an extra boost of thrust.*

### Turboprop

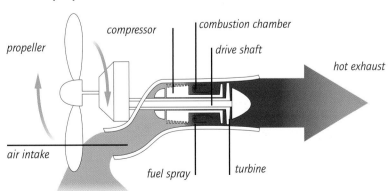

*propeller*
*compressor*
*combustion chamber*
*drive shaft*
*hot exhaust*
*air intake*
*fuel spray*
*turbine*

► *Turboprop engines use the rotation of the turbine to spin a conventional propeller, which helps to push the aircraft along. Turboprops are fuel efficient but can only be used by low-speed aircraft.*

▲ *The Bell X-1 design was a "bullet with wings," built to punch through the shockwave.*

chambers. In practice this resulted in a few heartstopping moments as Yeager struggled to gain control of the X-1.

On a crystal clear October 14, 1947, Yeager punched in the rocket engines of the X-1 over Rogers Dry Lake, southern California, and went on to earn himself a well-deserved place in history as the first person ever to fly faster than the speed of sound. At 43,000 ft (13,100 m) Yeager flew through the sound barrier at 662 mph (1,066 km/h).

## Aircraft after World War II

Today many military aircraft can travel faster than the speed of sound. The aim of the civilian jet designers, however, has been to build ever larger aircraft capable of carrying huge numbers of fare-paying passengers long distances for the least possible cost. On the whole, civilian airplane manufacturers have not been particularly interested in getting passengers to their destinations in the shortest possible time. Among designers of military airplanes, however, especially those producing fighters, speed and maneuverability are of the essence.

## SCIENTIFIC PRINCIPLES

### Traveling faster than sound

The speed of sound varies according to the air pressure. At 40,000 ft (12,100 m), where the air is not very dense, the speed of sound, or Mach 1, is 657 mph (1,060 km/h).

**1** When an airplane flies slower than the speed of sound, the pressure waves it makes travel at Mach 1 and radiate in front of and behind the airplane.

**2** When an airplane reaches Mach 1, the air flowing over its surfaces begins to form shock waves as the plane catches up with its own pressure waves. With these shock waves comes an incredible degree of turbulence.

**3** As the aircraft moves into supersonic speeds (above Mach 1), the shock waves form into a cone that causes a sonic boom to be heard for many miles around when it makes contact with the ground.

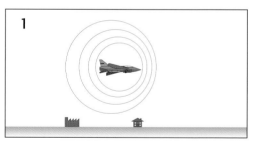

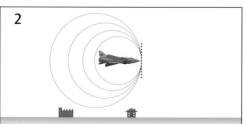

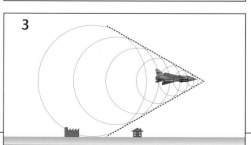

# HELICOPTERS

Before the beginning of the 20th century, the helicopter was merely a fascinating concept just waiting for engines light enough and powerful enough to drive it. A helicopter is a flying machine that creates lift with a spinning wing, or rotor. Airfoils create lift by air rushing around them at high speed. Fixed wings do this by powering down a runway, while a helicopter's spinning rotor rushes through the air while the rest of the aircraft stays in one place. This method allows helicopters to rise straight up into the from a small pad, not a long runway, and hover in one place in the air.

The earliest known reference to a rotor-powered flying machine appears in a Chinese text dated A.D. 320. It was not until 1907, however, that the very first piloted helicopter lifted off (although that was all it did, being capable only of vertical motion). The first practical—and steerable—helicopter was introduced, in the United States, by Russian-born U.S. engineer Igor Sikorsky (1889–1972; see inset picture below) in 1939.

In the 1950s engineers adapted the jet engine for use in helicopters, enabling them to travel farther and faster. Helicopters were used in the Korean War (1950–1953), but truly became practical aircraft in the Vietnam War (1957–1975), when Bell UH-1 transport helicopters (or "Hueys") were used to carry troops into battle.

▼ *The ability of a helicopter to hover in the air makes it a very useful flying machine. Rescue helicopters equipped with winches are the fastest way to get people out of danger.*

By the end of the Korean War (1950–1953) military aircraft manufacturers were making highly effective jet-powered fighters. Two notable examples, which met in battle over Korea, were the U.S. Air Force's F-86 Sabre and the former Soviet Union's MiG-15, which the Russians supplied to Korea.

Today's fast military jets employ the "turbojet" engine similar to Whittle's original design. However, civilian aircraft use the turbofan, which is a more efficient engine fitted with a large fan at the front end. This fan drives air around the engine to give more thrust—but limits the aircraft to subsonic speeds. Other types of jet include the turboprop engine—a jet turbine that turns a propeller—and the turboshaft, which is similar to the turboprop but is used to drive a helicopter's rotors.

## Stealth planes

As well as developing faster, more maneuverable aircraft, military designers need to make their planes harder for the enemy to locate. The result

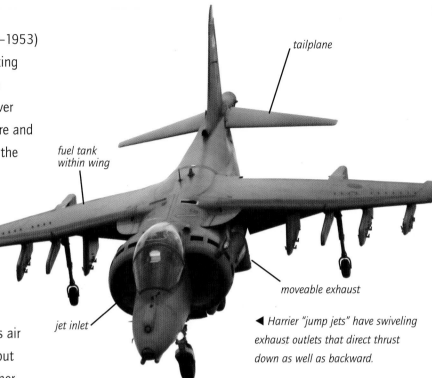

tailplane

fuel tank within wing

moveable exhaust

jet inlet

◀ Harrier "jump jets" have swiveling exhaust outlets that direct thrust down as well as backward.

---

## WORDS TO KNOW

- **Altitude:** The height above sea level.
- **Combustion:** When a substance burns.
- **Supersonic:** Faster than sound.
- **Turbine:** A series of propellers or fans that spin around when gases—or liquids—flow over them.

---

## V/STOL AIRCRAFT

Speed was not the only consideration when designing new aircraft. In 1954 the U.S. Navy developed the Convair XFY-1, the world's first plane that could perform a vertical takeoff. Known as the Pogo Stick, the XFY-1 stood on its tail while on the ground and took off straight up using propellers at the tip of the aircraft. In the air, the aircraft flew normally, but rotated upright again to land, slowly dropping on to its tail.

The Pogo Stick design was difficult to fly. A better V/STOL (Vertical/Short Take Off and Landing) plane was the Harrier "jump jet." A Harrier was powered by two compact jet engines. During normal flight the jets pointed backward, but could swivel to point down when the air craft needed to hover in the air, or rise straight up or down for takeoff and landing without a runway. Jump jets were ideal for use in rugged areas and on board ships. The F-35B Lightning, due to enter service in 2014, has a V/STOL engine for landing on aircraft carriers.

## V-22 Osprey: Half plane, half helicopter

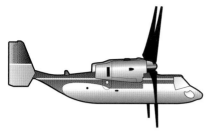

*1.* The aircraft's rotors point upward for a vertical takeoff.

*2.* Once in the air, the pilot swivels the rotors around.

*3.* The rotors are positioned at the tips of the wings, and when they are facing to the front the Osprey flies forward like other airplanes.

# SOCIETY AND INVENTIONS

## Airliners in the jet age

While Chuck Yeager was busy blazing a trail across the skies of southern California, manufacturers of civilian aircraft were just beginning to investigate the new technology that the war had produced. Without the stimulus of a world war, the civilian arm of the aircraft industry was lagging behind its uniformed companion. As economies began to recover, however, aircraft manufacturers looked to the growing market in international air travel as the way forward. In a calculated gamble, the British aircraft industry decided to concentrate on the production of innovative (and hopefully profitable) civilian passenger aircraft. Unable to compete against the mighty piston-engined airplanes from U.S. companies Lockheed and Douglas, such as the DC-7 (viewed by many as the pinnacle of piston-engine technology), British companies began to investigate the possibility of fitting a jet engine to a passenger airplane.

In 1952 the British-based company de Havilland introduced the first jet airliner—the de Havilland Comet. The initial reaction to this among U.S. aircraft manufacturers was to adapt existing airplanes to jet

engines. But in 1958 Boeing introduced the 707, the first purpose-built U.S. jet airliner, which set the style for the immensely popular 7-series jets that were to follow it. Within 20 years jet-powered air travel was within the reach of millions, making widespread, affordable air travel possible for more people than ever before.

▲ *The largest passenger jet in service today is the A380 "superjumbo." Up to 850 passenger seats are arranged over two decks and the giant aircraft can fly 9,400 miles (15,200 km)—more than half-way round the world—in one go.*

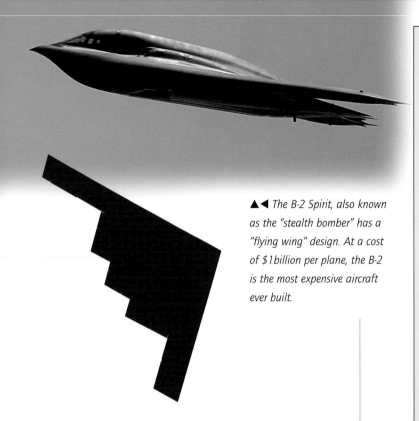

▲◄ The B-2 Spirit, also known as the "stealth bomber" has a "flying wing" design. At a cost of $1billion per plane, the B-2 is the most expensive aircraft ever built.

## SUPERSONIC AIRLINERS

While most military planes are supersonic, few civilian planes have been manufactured that can travel faster than the speed of sound. The first and only passenger-carrying supersonic airliner to come into service, in 1976, was Concorde—the result of a joint project between Britain and France. A fleet of 16 Concordes proved very expensive to operate and was banned from many airports because of the planes' loud sonic boom. In 2001 a Concorde crashed soon after takeoff in Paris, killing everyone on board. The other 15 planes were passed safe to continue flying, but the fleet was retired in 2003.

is "stealth" technology, a project initially set up by the U.S. government and Lockheed in 1980, and now used in all fields of military design, not just aircraft. Stealth aircraft are extremely difficult to detect using radar. This means that the aircraft need not be as fast or as maneuverable as other kinds of combat aircraft, since they are seldom attacked, and makes them ideal for surprise attacks.

The first stealth fighter was the Lockheed F-117 Nighthawk, a single-seater plane unveiled in 1983. The Northrop B-2 Spirit, a highly unusual stealth bomber shaped like a wing, became operational in 1989. The latest fighter in use by the U.S. Air Force, the F-22 Raptor, and the 5-35 Lightning which will enter service in 2014 are also stealth aircraft. It is said that

the twin-engine Raptor shows up as the size of a marble when scanned by radar, while the Lightning is easier to see—it's radar echo is the same size as one produced by a golf ball.

### High altitude and high speed

Another method of aircraft defense is not to avoid detection but just be beyond the range of weapons sent to attack. The Lockheed SR-71 Blackbird was a spyplane that operated between

## KEY COMPONENTS

### Stealth fighter

The shape of the Lockheed F-117 Nighthawk was kept a secret by the U.S. government until 1988. It was designed to be virtually undetectable by radar—especially at night and in cloudy weather. While the surfaces of normal airplanes are smooth and rounded for aerodynamic reasons, the surfaces of the F-117 are highly faceted (have many faces). Even the edges of the cockpit are jagged. This ensures that enemy radar is harmlessly deflected in several directions rather than reflected back to the enemy in a recognizable pattern. The engine air inlets are covered by grids to disperse enemy radar; and the jet nozzles are wide and flat so that the hot exhaust gases are spread out as they leave, making less of a target for heat-seeking missiles. Low detectability was achieved, however, at the expense of aerodynamics, speed, and maneuverability, making the F-117 a very difficult plane to fly. It has a digital control center to make steering easier, but pilots have still dubbed it the "wobbly goblin." The main advantage of the F-117 is in its ability to sneak up on a target (albeit slowly), take pictures or film, and launch a guided missile or smart bomb. However, the stealth plane was not immune from attack. In 1999, an F-117 was shot down by a missile targeted by human spotters on the ground.

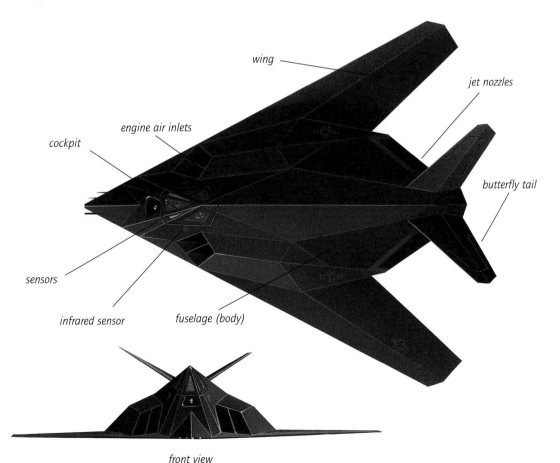

wing

jet nozzles

engine air inlets

cockpit

butterfly tail

sensors

infrared sensor

fuselage (body)

front view

▲ *An MQ-1 Predator is a pilotless "drone" aircraft powered by a propeller. Drones are used to spy on the enemy and fire weapons by remote control.*

the 1970s and 2000s. It could fly faster than Mach 3 and went so high that the pilot wore something similar to a spacesuit. The Blackbird holds the record for the fastest jet aircraft (2,193.2 mph; 3,529.6 km/h). If this plane was detected by an enemy, the pilot could easily outrun any surface-to-air missile launched to destroy it. Today's spy planes are pilotless "drones" that are easy to replace if destroyed and so do not need to fly fast or very high.

▼ *The F-35 Lightning is the latest fighter jet being developed for the US and UK air forces and navies. The first jets will be in service in 2014.*

## FACTS AND FIGURES

- The Bell X-1 had a single rocket engine, a maximum speed of 949 mph (1,531 km/h), and a wingspan of 28 ft (8.5 m).
- Concorde has four turbojet engines, a maximum speed of 1,380 mph (2,226 km/h), and a wingspan of 84 ft (25.6 m).
- Lockheed's F-117 Nighthawk (stealth fighter) has two turbofan (jet) engines, a maximum speed of 641 mph (1,034 km/h), and a wingspan of 43 ft (13 m).

### The future

It is not unusual for the developments in military aviation to be kept secret for several years after they have gone into action. It is likely that robot aircraft, piloted from a control room on the ground, will become more common in the air battles of the future. Civilian aircraft will become ever more efficient, using lightweight materials in place of metal bodies to save fuel, as airliners get bigger and fly for longer.

cockpit

engine air intake

body made from non-metal materials

undercarriage

## KEY COMPONENTS

### Combat helicopter

The helicopter shown here is the AH-64 Apache made by Boeing. It is an attack helicopter used by the U.S. military and by several other countries. The Apache is designed to operate above battlefields and needs to be fast but also highly maneuverable. It shares certain structural features with most helicopters. The tail and main rotor assemblies, which are driven by a turboshaft jet engine, are used to produce lift. Each rotor blade becomes an airfoil (a curved "wing" shape that generates lift)—as the blades spin around, the air pressure above the blade decreases while the pressure below the blade stays the same. This difference in pressure lifts the helicopter off the ground. Hinges in the rotor hub allow the pilot to alter each main rotor blade's pitch (angle) so that the craft can be steered. Increasing the pitch of the blades as they pass over the helicopter's nose, for example, makes the craft fly backward. This particular helicopter has a tailwheel; others have inflatable floats for water landing or skis for touching down on rough or soft ground.

The Apache has room for both a pilot and a gunner. The weapons are targeted using a system linked to the gunner's helmet. Wherever he or she looks, the laser guidance system follows, so missiles can hit whatever the crew can see.

▼ The Apache helicopter entered service in 1986. It has two engines mounted on either side of the aircraft. If one engine is damaged, the other is powerful enough to fly the helicopter to a safe landing area.

rotor blade

rotor hub

tail rotor

pilot

gunner

tailwheel

undercarriage

weapon-targeting system

# THE SPACE AGE

The story of flight does not end at the edge of the atmosphere. Spacecraft can leave Earth behind and fly in space. However, without any air to create lift, spaceflight required new inventions.

**Spacecraft are powered** by rockets. Only rockets work outside the atmosphere because unlike most other types of engine, they do not require oxygen from the air to burn their fuel.

The Chinese were using rockets as weapons as early as the 13th century, and they soon reached the Arab world. In the West, rockets were used most widely as fireworks, although they were briefly popularized as weapons by

▲ A Titan-Centaur rocket lifts off from Cape Kennedy Air Force Station in Florida in 1974.

## CONQUERING GRAVITY

The greatest barrier to space travel—and to flight in general—has always been gravity. Gravity is a force that attracts objects toward one another. The law of gravity, discovered by English physicist Isaac Newton (1643-1727), states that the strength of the force is determined by the mass of the two objects and the distance that separates them. When an object is released above the Earth (in midair), gravity pulls it toward the Earth. In order to remain airborne, an aircraft or spacecraft must produce an upward force (lift) greater than the downward force of gravity—but aircraft wings and engines will not work outside the atmosphere. At present, the only engine both powerful enough to get off the Earth and able to operate in the vacuum of space is the rocket.

## ROCKET PIONEER

Konstantin Tsiolkovsky (1857–1935), a Russian schoolteacher, was the first person to suggest using rockets to fly into space. He even proposed a liquid-fuel rocket powered by super-chilled liquid hydrogen and liquid oxygen—the fuels used by the largest rockets today.

Tsiolkovsky also invented the multistage rocket, which he called a "rocket train." To reach space, a rocket has to carry large amounts of fuel, but the larger the rocket is, the more it weighs, and the more empty weight it will be dragging with it as it reaches space. Multistage rockets have several segments of decreasing size. Each stage has its own liquid-fuel tanks and engine. The first and largest stage supplies the thrust to get the rocket off the ground, sometimes helped by solid- or liquid-fuel boosters. As the fuel in these early stages is exhausted, the stages are separated from the rest of the vehicle (jettisoned) and fall back to Earth. The rocket engines on the next stage then fire to carry the much lighter rocket farther into space. Although the upper stages carry less fuel than the first stage, they accelerate the vehicle much more quickly, because they are pushing a much-reduced weight.

British artillery officer Sir William Congreve (1772–1828). It was not until the 1890s that someone had the idea of using rockets in space.

Encouraged by the theories of Russian Konstantin Tsiolkovsky and others, many scientists became interested in rockets in the early 20th century. U.S. physics professor Robert Hutchings Goddard (1882–1945) was one such pioneer. He built the first practical liquid-fuel rockets and set many altitude records for rockets. During World War II (1939–1945) he worked on military uses for his rockets, but his designs were never put into service.

▼ *Fireworks, simple types of rockets invented in China, explode above a traditional Chinese building.*

## EARLY ROCKET DESIGNS

**1** Tsiolkovsky's first spaceship design of 1903 envisaged the use of liquid hydrogen as fuel and liquid oxygen as the oxidant, which provides the oxygen to burn the fuel. It also included exhaust vanes to steer the rocket by controlling the direction of the thrust.

**2** A crewed rocket was designed by Tsiolkovsky in 1911 in which the passenger lay face-upward on the floor of the top section. Today's rocket scientists have figured out that the curved combustion chamber in this design would have severely reduced the rocket's performance.

**3** Tsiolkovsky's rocket design of 1915 shows details of the valves that control the flow of fuel and oxidant into the combustion chamber. This design first appeared on the cover of Tsiolkovsky's 1935 book *Dreams of Earth and Sky*.

**4** The first liquid-fuel rocket to actually fly, designed by American Robert Goddard in 1926, used liquid oxygen as the oxidant and gasoline as the fuel.

**5** The "cone motor," designed by German engineer Hermann Oberth in 1929 and 1930, also burned liquid oxygen and gasoline. This simple rocket was widely used in German rocket experiments of the 1930s.

**6** Oberth's "Modell B" design, a two-stage rocket, was never built, but many of its features are incorporated in modern multistage rockets. The first stage uses liquid oxygen and alcohol as propellants, while the second stage uses liquid oxygen and liquid hydrogen as propellants. Modell B also had stabilizing fins to prevent the rocket from spinning in the air (this would have caused it to fly out of control).

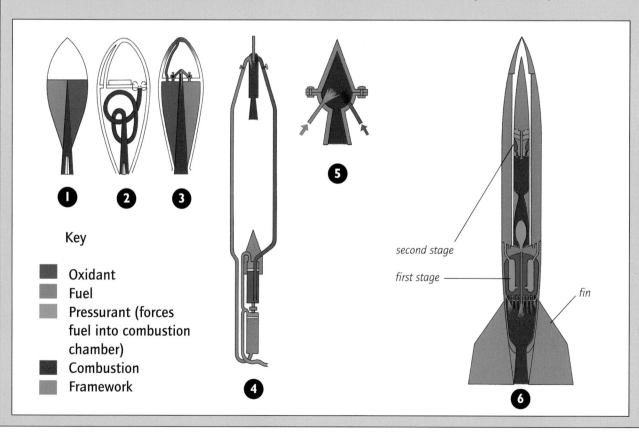

Key

■ Oxidant
■ Fuel
■ Pressurant (forces fuel into combustion chamber)
■ Combustion
■ Framework

second stage

first stage

fin

## SCIENTIFIC PRINCIPLES

### Rockets

Newton's third law of motion states that for every action there is an equal and opposite reaction. Rocket engines provide thrust using this principle. Substances (propellants) that move the rocket are burned in the combustion chamber, and the resulting hot exhaust gases escape through the cone-shaped nozzle at high speed. This action provides a force that propels the rocket in the opposite direction (the reaction). Rockets need two types of propellant: a fuel source and an oxidant, which provides oxygen to burn the fuel. Solid-fuel rockets usually consist of a metal cylinder packed with propellants with a nozzle at one end to let gases escape. The cylinder acts as the combustion chamber. Liquid-fuel rockets are more complex but easier to control. The fuel (often liquid hydrogen) and the oxidant (liquid oxygen) are stored in separate tanks and pumped into the combustion chamber by separate pumps. There the propellants are ignited, and the hot exhaust gases escape through the nozzle at rocket's base.

**Liquid-fueled rocket**

fuel tank

oxidizer tank

Liquids explode when they are mixed.

pumps

combustion chamber

nozzle

Jacket of cold liquid propellant used to keep engine nozzle cool.

**Solid-fueled rocket**

mixture of solid fuel and oxidizer

Igniter uses electric spark to set the fuel alight.

Fuel burns inside the hollow center.

nozzle

However, Germany had a highly successful rocket program throughout WWII. It was led by Wernher von Braun (1912–1977), who had been studying rocketry on a team led by German physics professor and rocket pioneer Hermann Oberth (1894–1989) since 1930. Von Braun's first rockets, the bomb-carrying V-2s, were launched at Britain, France, and Holland by Germany during WWII, but they did not alter the outcome of the war.

Sergei Korolev (1906–1966) was the great Russian pioneer of practical rocketry. In 1932 he became director of the Moscow Group Studying the Principles of Propulsion by Rocket Engines, and he launched the Soviet Union's (USSR's) first rocket one year later.

## The Space Race

On October 4, 1957, the USSR (an empire, now broken up, centered on Russia) shocked the world by announcing the successful launch of the satellite *Sputnik 1*. Radio listeners all over the world could pick up its distinctive "beep-beep" as it orbited the Earth. Shocked into action, the U.S. Army launched its first successful satellite, Explorer 1, in January 1958. Later that same year the National Aeronautics

▲ *A satellite radar image of the Arabian desert shows up features that are difficult to see from the ground. Colors have been added to show areas of rock (green), riverbed (white), and sand (blue and purple).*

### GPS SYSTEM

The Earth is also surrounded by a network of Navstar satellites 11,000 miles (17,700 km) up. These satellites are a part of the Global Positioning System (GPS). A GPS navigation device, such as one used by a driver, picks up several Navstar signals, and uses them to work out the positions of each satellites. From that the GPS device can figure out its exact position, to within a few feet.

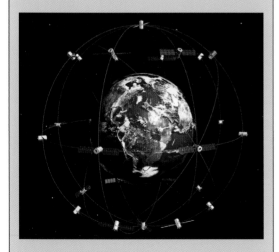

▲ *The constellation of Navstar satellites orbit Earth 12,552 miles (20,200 km) up.*

and Space Administration (NASA) was founded to coordinate the U.S. civilian space program.

Today there are many types of satellite in orbit. Communications satellites orbit farthest out, acting as relays for telephone calls, TV signals, and other information beamed around the world. Closer to Earth space becomes more crowded. Remote-sensing satellites study Earth from space, monitoring weather, searching for minerals, or spying on other countries. They orbit at altitudes of up to 625 miles (1,000 km), usually in polar orbits.

## FACTS AND FIGURES

### Orbits

**Low Earth Orbits** (LEOs), which are between 190–250 miles (300–400 km) up and parallel to the Earth's equator, are the easiest orbits to achieve because the rocket picks up extra speed from the Earth's own rotation. Satellites in this orbit circle the Earth in about 90 minutes.

**Elliptical orbits** are shaped like stretched circles, or pointed ovals. The satellite passes close to the Earth at one point and travels much farther out into space at another. Scientific satellites often use this type of orbit so that they can gather information on the conditions in space without interference from the Earth.

**Polar orbits** are orbits that pass over or near the poles. This type of orbit allows satellites to survey most of the surface of the Earth as it rotates under them. However, achieving this type of orbit requires a more powerful rocket than that needed to place a satellite in Low Earth Orbit.

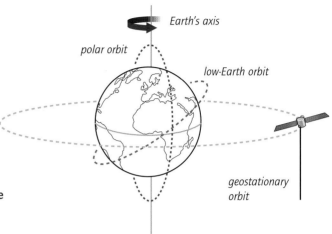

Earth's axis

polar orbit

low-Earth orbit

geostationary orbit

**The geostationary orbit** was worked out in 1945 by British science-fiction writer Arthur C. Clarke (born 1917). This is the orbit, 22,300 miles (35,900 km) above the equator, in which a satellite circles the Earth in precisely one day, always remaining above the same place on Earth. Weather satellites and those used in communications and broadcasting often have geostationary orbits.

## ARTIFICIAL SATELLITES

A satellite is an object that orbits a planet, held in place by the planet's gravitational field. The Moon is a natural satellite. Unlike airplanes artificial satellites do not have to be aerodynamic and can be virtually any shape and still function.

**1** The first artificial satellite, *Sputnik 1*, provided data on temperature and density in the upper atmosphere. Launched by the Soviet Union on October 4, 1957, it weighed 185 lb (84 kg). It flew around Earth in a low orbit 1,440 times before falling into the atmosphere and burning up.

**2** *Explorer 1* was the first successful U.S. satellite. It allowed scientists to discover that the Earth is girdled by bands of radiation held in place by the planet's magnetic field. Weighing 31 lb (14 kg), it was launched on January 31, 1958.

**3** *Sputnik 2* carried a dog, Laika, to study the biological effects of orbital flight. Laika traveled inside a pressurized cabin. Her heart rate and other signs of life were measured and sent back to Earth. *Sputnik 2* was launched on November 3, 1957, and weighed 1,120 lb (508 kg).

## People in space

As well as launching machines into orbit, scientists sent people to explore space. Sealed capsules with air supplies were first tested on animals, proving that living things could return from orbit alive. Some advances, however, could only be tested by putting real people in space.

▼ *The Freedom 7 spacecraft, atop a Mercury-Redstone (MR-3) rocket is launched from Cape Canaveral in 1961, Inside the black pod is Alan Shepard, the first American in space. Freedom 7 did not go into orbit but dropped back into the atmosphere after about three minutes in space.*

## FIRST SPACEMEN

In 1961, the first crewed spacecraft, the Soviet Union's *Vostok 1*, orbited the Earth with the first astronaut, Yuri Gagarin (1934-1968), on board. The craft was controlled by autopilot. The United States followed suit a few weeks after, putting first Alan Shepard (1923-1998) into space, and then John Glenn (born 1921), who became the first American to go into Earth orbit.

▲ *Yuri Gagarin prepares to board the rocket in 1961. His flight lasted just under two hours.*

The first human spaceflights were in 1961, and throughout the following decade crewed spaceflights became longer and more ambitious. The U.S. Gemini missions carried two men into space, sometimes staying in orbit for several days, and performed the first docking of two spacecraft. The Gemini missions also established how to move a spacecraft from one orbit to another by firing its rockets. If the rockets were used to increase the speed of the craft, it moved into a higher orbit. If retrorockets were used (these are rockets that fire in the same direction that the craft is moving to slow it down) the craft moved into a lower orbit.

## Weightlessness

An orbiting spacecraft is, in effect, continuously falling toward Earth, but since it is traveling forward at such high speeds, the Earth's surface curves away as the craft moves forward. Because both the spacecraft and its contents are moving at the same rate, there appears to be no gravity, resulting in the condition called weightlessness, microgravity, or zero gravity.

### FACTS AND FIGURES

**For a spacecraft** to travel farther than the Earth's atmosphere and reach orbit, it must be traveling at least 4.9 miles per second (7.8 km/s).

**For a spacecraft** to escape Earth's gravity altogether it must reach a velocity (speed) of at least 6.8 miles per second (11 km/s). This is called the escape velocity.

## SPACESUITS

The first spacesuits were modified versions of pressure suits worn by jet pilots, but they were reinvented in the mid-1960s to allow astronauts to leave their spacecraft and "spacewalk." A sealed outer suit made of airtight materials such as nylon and Teflon provides protection against heat, cold, radiation from the Sun, and tiny space particles called micrometeorites. Astronauts are often in very low-pressure environments, where the boiling point of the blood is normal body temperature. An inflatable inner layer of the spacesuit maintains a constant pressure on the body to prevent this happening. Excess heat is removed by water circulating in a network of tubes under the main suit. Tough outer layers provide protection, and folds in the material allow for limited movement. The backpack contains the life-support system that allow the wearer to breathe. NASA has also developed a rocket-powered suit used for flying independently around the main spacecraft.

Back on Earth, outfits similar to spacesuits have been designed for sufferers of rare light-sensitive disorders, enabling them to go outside in daylight for the first time.

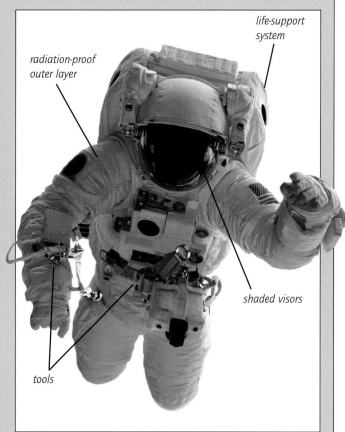

life-support system

radiation-proof outer layer

shaded visors

tools

## The race to the Moon

In 1961, U.S. President John F. Kennedy (1917–1963) announced NASA's Apollo Moon program, which had the goal of putting astronauts on the Moon by 1970.

The Apollo spacecraft had three modules. The command and service modules were designed to just orbit the Moon, from where the lunar module (LM) would separate and fly to the surface. The Apollo spacecraft were carried into space by a giant Saturn V rocket.

After a series of test runs, the Apollo 11 mission launched in July 16, 1969. On July 20,

with the Apollo capsule in orbit around the Moon, astronauts Buzz Aldrin (born 1930) and Neil Armstrong (born 1930) boarded the Eagle LM and separated from the orbiter, crewed by Michael Collins (born 1930). The LM had retrorockets to slow it down, and it made a perfect, soft landing in the Sea of Tranquility on the Moon. Neil Armstrong stepped out, becoming the first man on the Moon. In total 12 Americans, all men, visited the Moon. No one has been back since December 1972.

▼ Buzz Aldrin poses for a photograph on the Moon. His crew mate, Neil Armstrong (taking the picture), and the Lunar Module are reflected in Aldrin's mirror visor.

## KEY COMPONENTS

### Saturn V Moon rocket

The immense rocket had three stages, each with its own engines. The launch escape system was a small rocket that could take off separately in case of any mishaps during launch, carrying the crew in the command module to safety.

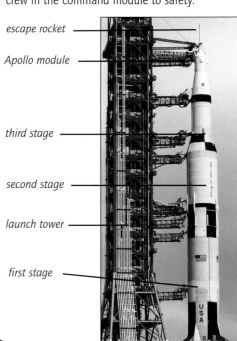

escape rocket

Apollo module

third stage

second stage

launch tower

first stage

# THE APOLLO MISSIONS

The Apollo missions were among the most complex and ambitious voyages ever. The diagram below shows the main stages of the trip to the Moon.

**1** Saturn V lifts off and enters orbit around the Earth.

**2** The Apollo spacecraft leaves orbit. The command and service module (CSM) separates and links to the lunar module (LM).

**3** LM and CSM enter orbit around the Moon using retrorockets, which fire in the same direction that the craft is traveling, to reduce speed.

**4** LM separates and prepares to land. CSM remains in orbit around Moon.

**5** LM uses radar to gauge its height and fires retrorockets to slow itself during its approach and soft landing on the lunar surface.

**6** LM ascent stage lifts off from the Moon and rejoins the CSM in orbit. All astronauts return to the CSM, which separates from the LM, leaving it to crash into the Moon, while the CSM sets a course back to Earth.

**7** The command module (CM) separates from the service module, which burns up in the atmosphere, while the CM re-enters the atmosphere and makes a safe splashdown in the Pacific Ocean, using parachutes to slow its fall.

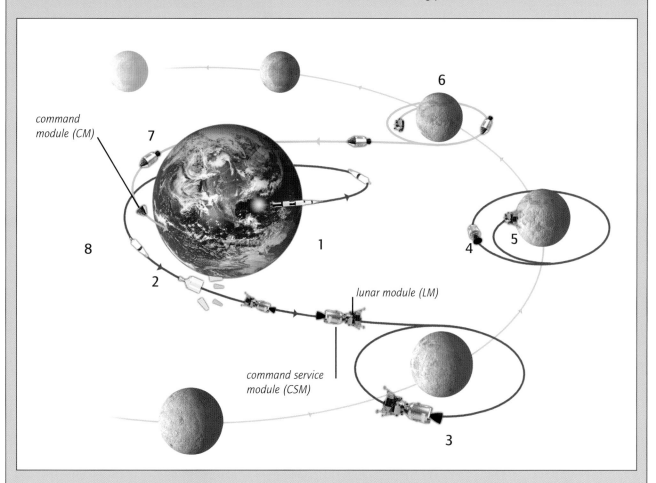

*command module (CM)*

*lunar module (LM)*

*command service module (CSM)*

## The space shuttle

The first space shuttle, *Columbia*, was launched in 1981. *Columbia* and its four sister ships, *Challenger*, *Discovery*, *Atlantis*, and *Endeavour*, were the backbone of the U.S. space program. They could carry out tricky satellite launches, repair and recovery missions, and even ferry a laboratory, Spacelab, into orbit. The shuttle made flying into space routine, but tragically *Challenger* exploded on launch in January 1986, killing the crew. Safety features were added, but in February 2003, *Columbia* was also destroyed as it re-entered the atmosphere. The shuttle program was ended in 2011, as NASA reverted to using rockets to send craft into space.

▶ *There were more than 130 space shuttle flights over 30 years of service. The shuttle that flew the most was* Discovery, *which lifted off 38 times.*

# SOCIETY AND INVENTIONS

## Space spinoffs

Space exploration has, at times, attracted criticism due to its enormous cost. However, many of the advances made by space scientists and engineers do find everyday uses. Many of these "spinoffs" are in the area of medicine. Advanced pacemakers for patients with irregular heartbeats have been developed using NASA's two-way communication technology, first used to communicate with satellites. Doctors can adjust these pacemakers from outside the body, improving the regulation of the patient's heartbeat. Surgical heart pumps based on aerospace engine pump technologies have also been developed. Astronauts who spend long periods in space can weaken their hearts and muscles. The Telemedicine Instrumentation Pack (TIP) was used on space shuttle missions to make physical examinations of the crew and send the results to doctors on Earth. A TIP can also be used in remote areas by people with little training to consult with medics in other locations, bringing healthcare to people with no local doctor.

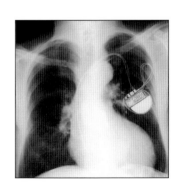

▶ *Thanks to space science modern pacemakers can be fine-tuned by doctors from outside the body.*

# A SPACE SHUTTLE MISSION

**1** Solid-fuel rocket boosters are strapped to an empty fuel tank on the mobile launch platform at the Vehicle Assembly Building (VAB) of the Kennedy Space Center.

**2** The orbiter is attached to the boosters and external tank, and the whole structure is moved to the launch complex.

**3** The external tank is filled with liquid hydrogen (in the bottom segment) and liquid oxygen (top). Takeoff is powered by the two boosters and the orbiter's three main rocket engines.

**4** Two minutes after takeoff, at an altitude (height) of 28 miles (45 km), the boosters separate.

**5** At an altitude of 68 miles (109 km), before orbit is reached, the main engines cut off and the external tank separates.

**6** Two smaller maneuvering rockets on the orbiter propel it into the required orbit.

**7** On the return to Earth the orbiter reverses its direction and fires main engines to slow the spacecraft down as it reenters the atmosphere.

**8** Back in Earth's atmosphere, the orbiter glides like an aircraft and comes to land on the runway, at speeds of up to 226 mph (364 km/h). After checks and repairs the orbiter can be used again.

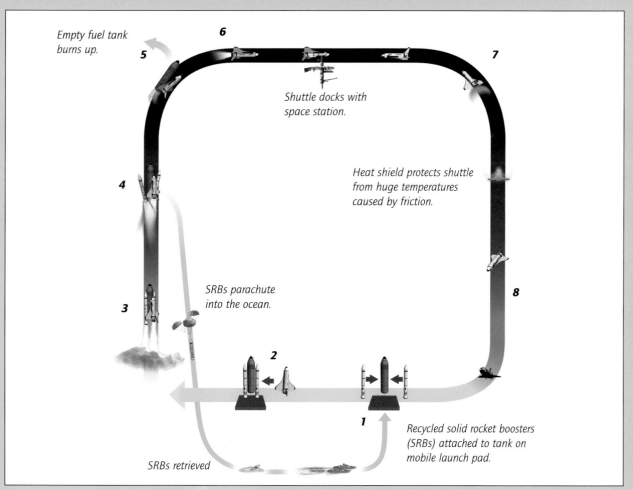

*Empty fuel tank burns up.*

*Shuttle docks with space station.*

*Heat shield protects shuttle from huge temperatures caused by friction.*

*SRBs parachute into the ocean.*

*SRBs retrieved*

*Recycled solid rocket boosters (SRBs) attached to tank on mobile launch pad.*

▲ Electricity for space stations is provided by large solar panels, or arrays. These use the energy from the Sun to create an electric current. The International Space Station's solar arrays would cover half a football field.

## Space stations

In the 1970s, NASA and its rival Soviet space agency turned their attentions to building satellites that were large enough and equipped for crews to live in them for long periods, even permanently. The space station was born. Space stations are used largely as laboratories, where experiments can be performed in weightlessness and the vacuum of space.

The USSR launched the first station, Salyut 1, in 1971. This was followed by six further Salyuts and finally, in 1986, the Mir space station. Meanwhile, NASA created the Skylab project, based on technology developed during the Apollo missions. Skylab was visited by three missions during 1973 before burning up in Earth's atmosphere in 1979.

## SPACE STATION DESIGNS

Space stations contain everything needed to keep a crew in space for a long time. For example, Salyut 1 consisted of four modules. At one end was a propulsion unit with small rockets for moving the station in its orbit. The two middle pods had beds, workshops, and exercise equipment—astronauts have to exercise regularly to prevent their muscles wasting away in the weightlessness of space. At the other end was an airlock and docking port, where the astronauts' spacecraft was attached. Later space stations had two docking ports, allowing automatic supply capsules or visiting astronauts to dock. Since two craft could dock at the same time, the station did not have to be left unoccupied between missions.

Space laboratories have been used to produce perfect crystals and other materials undistorted by gravity, and to study the effects of weightlessness on plants and animals. In the future it may be economical to manufacture some materials and medicines in space and return them to Earth.

## SOCIETY AND INVENTIONS

### Space tourists

In 2004, the first private spacecraft, *SpaceShipOne* was launched into space. In October that year, the rocket plane became the first craft to fly into space twice in just two weeks. Now the same launch system is being developed for taking paying passengers into space. A larger model, called *SpaceShipTwo*, has room for six passengers and two pilots. The spacecraft is carried to 50,000 ft (15,000 m) underneath a jet-powered mothership (*White Knight Two*) before being released and powering to an altitude of 62 miles (100 km) using its rocket. After a few minutes in space, *SpaceShipTwo* glides back to the ground.

In 1998 construction of the International Space Station (ISS) began, a joint venture between many of the world's main space agencies, including NASA, the Russian Space Agency, and the European Space Agency (ESA), with smaller contributions from many other countries. The ISS has been permanently crewed with at least two astronauts since October 2000. The station will be completed in 2012 and is due to keep working until at least 2020.

### Spaceflight today

The future of human spaceflight is uncertain. Plans for a crewed mission to the Moon in 2020 have been cancelled and there are no plans to replace the space shuttle with a similar crewed orbiter. Crews of all nationalities heading to the ISS lift off from the Star City complex in Kazakhstan. They travel in *Soyuz* modules, a Russian spacecraft design that was first used in the 1960s. China has also developed the *Shenzhou* spacecraft, which carried the first Chinese astronaut into orbit in 2003.

The latest American spacecraft is the *X-37*, an uncrewed shuttle with a small cargo bay, launched on top of a rocket. In its first flight in 2010, the *X-37* orbited for eight months before gliding back to Earth under remote control.

# EXPLORING OTHER WORLDS

The Space Age has allowed people to explore other planets and the farthest reaches of the Solar System. The distances involved are too great for human crews so robots and remote-controlled craft are sent in their place.

**For thousands of years** the other planets in our Solar System were mysterious, distant objects. For the past few centuries we have known that they are actually other worlds, but until very recently these worlds could only be studied by astronomers using telescopes on Earth. Our study of the larger Universe has also

▲ *A montage of the Saturn system, showing the planet and its main moons. The images put together to create this picture were taken by space probes.*

been held back by the atmosphere, which distorts and absorbs starlight.

The Space Age has changed all of this. Since the 1950s dozens of astronomical satellites have been put into orbit, where they can study light from the Universe in the vacuum of space. Even more ambitiously, we have sent space probes to all of the planets in our Solar System and beyond, into interstellar space.

The first Soviet astronomical satellite, *Sputnik 3*, was launched in May 1958. This

# LANDING ON THE MOON

The early Moon probes were crude devices designed to return data before crashing into the lunar surface. Landing a probe safely on the Moon was more difficult. Navigation and control had to be improved so that the probe could be placed on a suitable landing site (a relatively flat, firm plain), and additional rockets were needed to reduce the craft's speed as it neared the surface (the Moon has no atmosphere, so parachutes could not be used to slow the descent). These features added to the weight of the probe, so a more powerful rocket was needed to launch it. The first probe to make a soft landing on the Moon was *Luna 9*, launched by the USSR in January 1966. The probe took photographs and measured radiation, returning data to Earth by radio. NASA's *Surveyor I* probe landed on the Moon four months later. Instead of sending people to the Moon, the Soviet Space Agency used a series of sophisticated probes to gather scientific data and return samples of Moon rock to Earth.

▲ *Luna 9* was the first spacecraft to land on the Moon.

◄ *Astronaut Charles Conrad, checks out* Surveyor III, *a moon probe that had landed a couple of years before the the Apollo spacecraft (top right) arrived in 1969.*

# SATELLITE DISCOVERY

The very first successful U.S. satellite, *Explorer 1*, carried an astronomical instrument—a radiation detector—built by James van Allen (1914-2006) of Iowa University. Van Allen hoped to study high-energy "cosmic rays," which almost never reach the Earth's surface. But when *Explorer 1* was launched in January 1958, the radiation detector went wild as the satellite orbited through certain regions. These were areas of trapped radiation and were named the "Van Allen Belts."

mission also carried a radiation detector and had an elliptical (stretched) orbit that allowed it to measure both the Van Allen Belts and cosmic rays in more distant space. *Sputnik 3* also pioneered a new communications system that permitted data to be stored over the entire orbit then transmitted or "dumped" to ground stations as the satellite passed over the USSR.

From these small beginnings both NASA and the Soviet Space Agency launched many more satellites. Scientific satellites are one area of space in which scientists of many nations collaborate. Each satellite can carry many separate instruments and experiments, and these are often built at colleges and research institutes in countries that have no space programs of their own.

### Probes to the Moon

The first spacecraft to reach the Moon was *Luna 2*, an uncrewed Soviet probe launched in 1959. A powerful rocket lifted the probe out of Earth orbit, and the precise timing of the launch meant that the probe swung onto a collision course with the Moon. *Luna 2* carried a range of scientific instruments and transmitted data back

## SOCIETY AND INVENTIONS

### Life on Mars?

The idea that there might be life on Mars has fascinated people for hundreds of years. Ground-based telescopes were not powerful enough to shed much light on the debate, although some astronomers thought that they could see great networks of canals—presumably built by some alien civilization—on the planet's surface. In his novel *War of the Worlds*, English writer H.G. Wells (1866-1946) described the Martians as a chilling race intent on capturing Earth. The reality, however, is less dramatic—the Viking probes, which visited Mars in 1976, found no evidence of canals or living things on the planet's dusty surface.

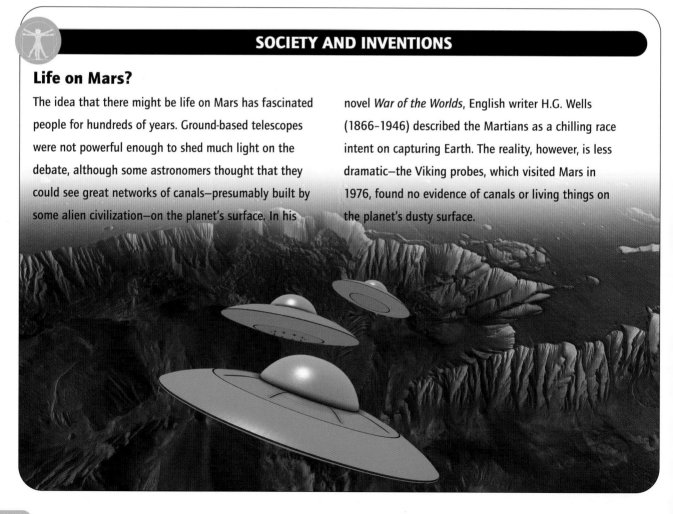

to Earth via a radio link. *Luna 3*, launched one month later, was even more successful, returning the first pictures of the far side of the Moon. Digital cameras had yet to be invented, and so the probe took a video with a film camera. The film was developed and processed on board before being scanned and transmitted to Earth by radio. The picture quality was very poor, but

## MARINER MISSIONS

The Mariner probes were the first spacecraft to be sent to visit another planet. *Mariner 2* (above) flew past Venus (the nearest planet to Earth) in December 1962. The probe's electrical power was provided by solar panels, and it was also equipped with a rocket engine for course corrections, sensors, cameras, and an array of scientific equipment. JPL scientists sent commands to the probe by radio. The probe used radio waves to look through Venus's thick clouds, revealing a hellish surface with temperatures of around 750°F (400°C).

NASA's next goal, a visit to Mars, was achieved by *Mariner 4* in July 1965. Throughout the rest of the 1960s and into the 1970s further Mariner probes visited both Mars and Venus—*Mariner 9* actually went into orbit around Mars in 1971 and sent back detailed photographs of the planet's surface.

In 1974, *Mariner 10* became the first and only probe to visit Mercury. It flew via Venus, and used that planet's gravity to swing the probe onto a course past Mercury. This technique is called the gravity slingshot. *Mariner 10* also became a test vehicle for an even more revolutionary idea—the solar sail. By altering the tilt of Mariner's solar panels, JPL scientists made the probe "sail" between orbits, propelled by the solar wind—a continuous stream of charged particles radiating from the Sun.

## KEY COMPONENTS

### Viking orbiters and landers

The Viking probes gave scientists their first close-up look at the surface of Mars. The two probes were the most ambitious spacecraft constructed by NASA since Apollo. Each consisted of an orbiter based on Mariner spacecraft and a lander derived from the Surveyor Moon probes. The spacecraft weighed 7,758 lb (3,519 kg) at launch and were propelled out of Earth orbit by powerful Atlas-Centaur rockets. A computer on the orbiter then took over control of the spacecraft, using the positions of the Sun and the star Canopus to navigate. Information on the probe's position and status was relayed back to Earth by radio using the communications antenna. The probe was controlled by an on-board computer rather than an operator on Earth because radio signals (traveling at the speed of light) take almost 20 minutes to reach Mars from Earth. As the spacecraft approached Mars, the propulsion motor was fired, placing the vehicle in a stable orbit. The lander then separated from the orbiter

and descended to the Martian surface, using parachutes and rockets to slow its fall. The orbiter completed a comprehensive study of the planet from space using two television cameras, a thermal mapper that could determine the surface and atmospheric temperatures, and a water-vapor detector that measured the amount of water in the Martian atmosphere. The *Viking* lander carried cameras and equipment to measure weather and earthquakes. Its most important mission, however, was to search for signs of life. This involved collecting Martian soil with the sample collection boom and depositing it in the organic molecule detector. Moisture and nutrients were added to start any life processes, and changes in the sample chemistry were recorded. Some changes did occur, but scientists think that these were probably not due to living organisms.

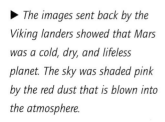
▶ The images sent back by the Viking landers showed that Mars was a cold, dry, and lifeless planet. The sky was shaded pink by the red dust that is blown into the atmosphere.

Soviet scientists were able to enhance the images using early computers.

Meanwhile, NASA was developing its own series of Moon probes—the Rangers, designed to crash into the lunar surface, sending pictures and other data back to Earth in preparation for Apollo missions, which would take men to the Moon.

## Missions to Venus and Mars

The Earth is one of four small, rocky inner planets. The other three—Mercury, Venus, and Mars—are our nearest neighbors in space and were the obvious next targets for space probes. NASA's Mariner spacecraft were among the first probes to fly past and orbit these planets in the 1960s and 1970s.

In the 1980s, NASA designed spacecraft to take an even closer look at our neighboring planets. Before this, most probes had been limited to high-speed "flybys," snatching a brief snapshot at the alien world and its moons. To obtain data over many months, a probe must go into orbit around the planet or even land on it.

NASA's *Magellan* orbiter spent three years circling Venus, starting in 1990. To look through the thick clouds, it carried radar equipment used by remote-sensing satellites to map the Earth. Scientists were able to turn this information into detailed maps of the planet's surface.

▶ The Opportunity *rover landed on Mars in 2004, a short while after its sister probe,* Spirit, *landed on the other side of the planet. The probes were powered by solar arrays.* Spirit *operated for more than five years, while* Opportunity *is still actively exploring the red planet.*

◀ *The surface of Venus mapped by the* Magellan *probe between 1990 and 1994. The probe then fell out of orbit, broke apart, and crashed into the planet's surface,*

In 1997, the Mars Pathfinder mission delivered a small rover, called *Sojourner*, to Mars, the "red planet." The six-wheeled, solar-powered rover hit the surface inside a cocoon of large airbags which inflated once the lander had entered the atmosphere to break the fall. In December 2003, a larger probe called *Spirit* landed on Mars using the same system. (An identical rover, *Opportunity*, arrived a few weeks later in 2004.)

The Mars rovers were sent commands by radio from the NASA control center, which took

cameras

radio transmitter

solar panels

metal wheel

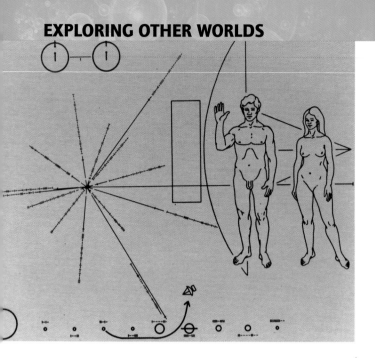

▲ The Voyager and Pioneer probes carried a plaque showing who had made them and where they came from—just in case they were ever found by an alien civilization. The Voyagers also carried a gold audio disc that contained the sounds of animals, wind, the ocean, 90-minutes of music, and greetings spoken in 55 Earth languages.

a lot of careful planning because of the long communication delay. The rovers sent back detailed pictures of Mars's surface and analyzed the chemicals in the Martian soil using on-board automatic laboratories.

In 2008, the *Phoenix* probe made a soft landing on Mars. A parachute deployed and retrorockets fired according to a pre-programmed schedule to slow the craft down for a safe landing. *Phoenix* was equipped with a shovel for digging into the soil. The probe dug up lumps of water ice, showing that Mars is not as dry as previously thought.

### To the outer planets

The way to the outer planets was opened up by the Pioneer and Voyager probes launched by NASA in the 1970s. *Pioneer 10*, the first probe

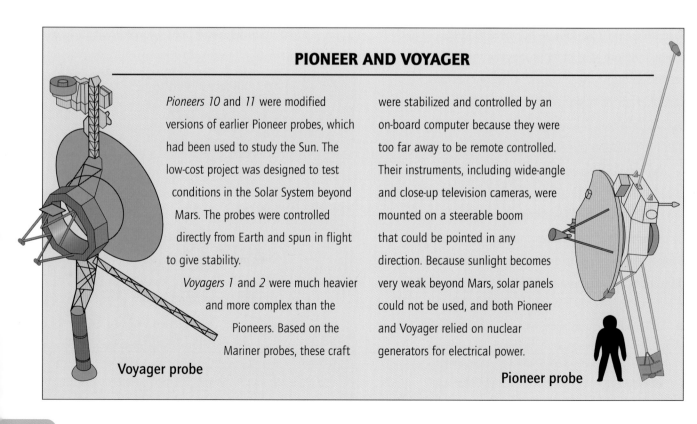

## PIONEER AND VOYAGER

*Pioneers 10* and *11* were modified versions of earlier Pioneer probes, which had been used to study the Sun. The low-cost project was designed to test conditions in the Solar System beyond Mars. The probes were controlled directly from Earth and spun in flight to give stability.

*Voyagers 1* and *2* were much heavier and more complex than the Pioneers. Based on the Mariner probes, these craft were stabilized and controlled by an on-board computer because they were too far away to be remote controlled. Their instruments, including wide-angle and close-up television cameras, were mounted on a steerable boom that could be pointed in any direction. Because sunlight becomes very weak beyond Mars, solar panels could not be used, and both Pioneer and Voyager relied on nuclear generators for electrical power.

**Voyager probe**

**Pioneer probe**

## LANDING ON SATURN'S MOON

In 1997, the *Cassini-Huygens* mission lifted off from Cape Canaveral, Florida, and set course to Saturn. The mission was a joint venture between NASA and ESA, the European Space Agency. The spacecraft took a slingshot around Venus and flew past Jupiter at the end of 2000. The nuclear-powered probe reached the Saturn system in 2004, even flying through a gap in the rings. The mission was named for two scientists, Frenchman Giovanni Domenico Cassini and Dutchman Christiaan Huygens, both of whom made early descriptions of Saturn's rings and moons in the 17th century. In 2005, the *Huygens* lander touched down on the surface of Titan, Saturn's largest moon. It found a world covered in frozen methane and oceans of gasoline-like chemicals.

▶ The Huygens *lander was dropped by the* Cassini *orbiters as it flew past Titan, and spent three weeks approaching the planet. The lander floated to the surface by parachute.*

to visit Jupiter, arrived in 1973. *Pioneer 11* passed Jupiter one year later and used the planet's gravity to swing it on to a course for Saturn, which it reached in 1979. *Voyager 1* made the same journey, reaching Jupiter in 1979 and Saturn in 1980. *Voyager 2* took advantage of a rare alignment of all the gas giant planets—Jupiter, Saturn, Uranus, and Neptune—and visited each planet in turn. Both Voyagers carried television cameras that returned brilliant color photographs of the planets and moons that they encountered.

*Galileo*, which arrived at Jupiter in 1995, was a two-part probe. An orbiter surveyed the planet and its moons, while a probe dropped

### FACTS AND FIGURES

This table gives the distances of the eight planets of the Solar System (and the dwarf planet Pluto) from the Sun.

| Mercury | 36 million miles | (58 million km) |
|---|---|---|
| Venus | 67 million miles | (108 million km) |
| Earth | 93 million miles | (150 million km) |
| Mars | 142 million miles | (228 million km) |
| Jupiter | 483 million miles | (778 million km) |
| Saturn | 886 million miles | (1,427 million km) |
| Uranus | 1,783 million miles | (2,870 million km) |
| Neptune | 2,794 million miles | (4,497 million km) |
| Pluto | 3,666 million miles | (5,900 million km) |

## SCIENTIFIC PRINCIPLES

### Ion engines

All rockets work on the same principle: they expel matter in one direction, and this pushes the rocket in the opposite direction. Chemical rockets expel hot exhaust gases but ion rockets expel a stream of ions (charged particles). Ion engines provide a lot less thrust than other rockets (they cannot launch a probe from Earth) but are ideal for long journeys because they are very fuel efficient.

Ion rocket engines use electricity generated by solar panels to power their heating coils and other structures. The heating coils change the fuel into a gas.

The gas xenon, stored in the fuel tank in liquid form, is the fuel used by the probe *Deep Space 1*. A hot metallic grid then removes parts of the atoms (minute particles that make up all matter, including gases), turning them into positively charged particles called ions. The ions are focused into a stream, and then an electric field accelerates them from the rocket.

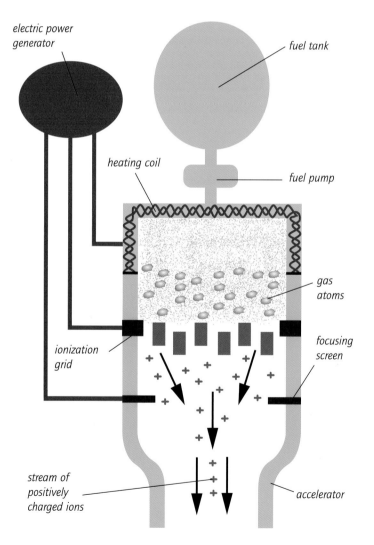

electric power generator

fuel tank

heating coil

fuel pump

gas atoms

ionization grid

focusing screen

stream of positively charged ions

accelerator

▼ Deep Space 1, *the probe powered by an ion engine, flew past the asteroid 9969 Braille in 1999, before changing course and visiting Borrelly's Comet in 2001.*

into Jupiter's atmosphere, returning data before it was destroyed by pressure and heat.

## Other missions

In 2001, *NEAR Shoemaker* became the first spacecraft to land on an asteroid, touching down on Eros, a giant rock that orbits close to Earth. In 2010, Japan's *Hayabusa* probe brought back dust from the asteroid Itokawa for analysis on Earth. In 2006, the *New Horizons* mission set off to study the outer edge of the Solar System.

▶ *After visiting Pluto and its moons in 2015,* New Horizons *may travel on to the Kuiper Belt, a region filled with bodies of ice. Many comets come from this area.*

## COMETS PROBE

▲ Giotto *sent back the first close-up pictures of the core, or nucleus, of Halley's Comet, showing the plumes of hot gas and plasma that erupt from the 7-mile (11-km) wide ball of ice.*

When Halley's Comet flew past the Earth in 1986, there was a huge international mission to study it. Halley's Comet is the only bright comet that returns often (every 76 years or so), and so missions to it can be planned in advance. The European Space Agency's *Giotto* probe (left) carried a camera and several scientific instruments and flew within a few hundred miles of the comet's core. The spacecraft's base was covered by a thick shield made from Kevlar, an extremely strong plastic (used in bulletproof vests). This shield protected the probe as it entered the dust cloud produced by the comet's interaction with the Sun. *Giotto* also carried batteries that could provide electrical power to its experiments if its solar panel was damaged.

**1783** Marquis d'Arlandes and François Pilâtre de Rozier become the first aviators, flying 5.5 miles (9 km) over Paris in a hot-air balloon made by the Montgolfier brothers.

**1783** A few months after the Montgolfier flight, fellow Frenchman, Jacques-Alexandre Charles flew to an altitude of nearly 1 mile (1.6 km), in the first hydrogen balloon.

**1804** Sir George Cayley constructs the first working model of a fixed-wing aircraft.

**1852** Frenchman Henri Giffard builds the first airship, or dirigible, powered by a steam engine.

**1853** A full-size glider built by George Cayley carries a person on a short flight.

**1896** Otto Lillienthal dies in a glider crash.

**1903** Bicyclemakers Wilbur and Orville Wright achieve the world's first controlled flight in a powered airplane.

**1903** Schoolteacher Konstantin Tsiolkovsky suggests using rockets to reach space.

**1907** The monoplane is invented by Louis Blériot; he later uses it to fly across the English Channel.

**1910** Romanian engineer Henri Coanda builds a prototype aircraft that is powered by a jet of air. It never flies.

**1912** American Glenn Curtiss builds the first flying boat, the *Flying Fish*.

**1919** British airmen John Alcock and Arthur Brown fly across the Atlantic in a biplane.

**1929** Robert Goddard launches the first liquid-fueled rocket.

**1929** The *Graf Zeppelin* airship makes the first round the world flight, taking a little more than 21 days.

**1930** Frank Whittle patents the jet engine.

**1933** Boeing designs the first modern airliner, the 247.

**1937** The *Hindenburg*, a hydrogen-filled airship explodes in New Jersey, killing many of its passengers. Airships are rarely used again.

**1939** The first jet-powered airplane, the Heinkel He-178, is flown.

**1939** The first practical helicopter is flown in the United States by engineer Igor Sikorsky.

**1947** Chuck Yeager is the first person to fly through the sound barrier in the Bell *X-1*.

**1954** The Convair XFY-1 Pogo Stick becomes the first V/STOL aircraft, followed later by the Harrier jump jet and V-22 Osprey.

**1957** The first artificial satellite, *Sputnik I*, is launched by the Soviet Union.

**1961** The USSR (now the Russian Federation) launches the first passenger-carrying spacecraft with astronaut Yuri Gagarin on board. American Alan Shepard is launched into space a few weeks later.

**1962** *Telstar*, the first working communications satellite, is launched.

**1962** The *X-15* rocket plane flies at Mach 5, five times the speed of sound.

**1969** NASA launches Apollo 11, the first successful crewed mission to the Moon.

**1971** *Mariner 9* becomes the first spacecraft to go into orbit around another planet.

**1976** The Lockheed SR-71 becomes the fastest jet-powered aircraft, flying faster than Mach 3.

**1983** The "stealth" fighter, or F-117 Nighthawk, is built by Lockheed.

**1989** *Voyager II* passes Neptune, the outermost planet in the Solar System.

**1998** Construction of the International Space Station (ISS) begins.

**2001** The first tourist visits space. American Dennis Tito pays $20 million for 9 days aboard the ISS.

**2004** *SpaceshipOne* is the first reusable space-craft to fly into space twice in 14 days. A similar craft is planned to carry tourists into space.

**2004** The *Opportunity* rover lands on Mars.

**2010** The Japanese *Hayabusa* probe returns the first asteroid dust to Earth.

# GLOSSARY

**aerodynamic** Able to move through a fluid (such as air) efficiently. Aerodynamic objects are shaped to reduce drag.

**airfoil** A shaped surface, typically curved on one side and straight on the other, that produces both lift and drag when moved through the air. Airplane wings and propellers are examples of airfoils.

**altitude** The height of an aircraft or spacecraft measured above sea level.

**ancient Greece** A civilization that existed on the mainland and islands of modern-day Greece and Turkey between 2000 and 300 B.C.

**asteroid** A space rock that orbits the Sun. Most of the asteroids in the solar system orbit in the Asteroid Belt located between the orbits of Mars and Jupiter.

**atom** The smallest units in any substance.

**aviator** A person who flies an aircraft.

**combustion** When a substance burns. Engines burn fuel in combustion chambers.

**compression** The act of being made more compact by the application of pressure.

**dense** A description of how much mass is packed into a substance. A handful of a dense substance, such as lead, weighs a lot. The same amount of hydrogen, which has a very low density, weighs much less.

**drag** A force that opposes the motion of an object through a fluid such as air or water.

**drone** An aircraft that has no passengers or crew, but is flown by a pilot on the ground.

**fuselage** The body of an airplane, containing the cockpit and passenger cabin. The earliest aircraft had a basic frame for a fuselage. Modern planes use super-strong plastics and metals.

**gravity** A natural force that attracts two masses toward one another. Among its many effects, gravity draws objects toward Earth's surface and keeps the planets in orbit around the Sun.

**hydrogen** A highly flammable gas that is lighter than air. Pure hydrogen is uncommon on Earth. It is manufactured by breaking up water molecules into hydrogen and oxygen gas.

**internal combustion** The engine system used in cars and trucks, fueled by gasoline or diesel. Propeller planes use large internal-combustion engines.

**interstellar** Referring to the empty space between star systems. There are few large objects, such as planets or asteroids, in interstellar space. It is the emptiest place in the Universe.

**Korean War (1950–1953)** A war in which a U.S.-dominated United Nations coalition came to the aid of South Korea during an invasion by North Korea, which was aided by the Soviet Union and communist China. The war was ultimately indecisive and the two countries are still technically at war with each other, although fighting is relatively rare.

**Mach 1** The speed that sound travels through air in current conditions. The speed varies according to the temperature and pressure of the air, so Mach 1 is not a set figure. Mach 2 refers to double the speed of Mach 1.

This numbering system is named for German scientist Ernst Mach (1838–1916).

**microgravity** The term used to describe weightlessness in space. Gravity is still acting on astronauts and the objects inside the spacecraft, but its effect in them is too small to notice.

**orbit** The path, shaped like a circle or an ellipse, that an object in space takes around another object.

**ramjet** A jet engine that does not have a turbine, but produces thrust as a stream of exhaust gases by burning fuel in a stream of air drawn in the front. Ramjets work best at very high speeds.

**remote sensing** The measuring of electromagnetic radiation. Remote-sensing devices, often mounted on aircraft or satellites, usually detect electromagnetic waves reflected from the surface of Earth.

**satellite** A natural or artificial object in orbit around a star, planet, or other body.

**solar panels** Collections of solar cells used to convert sunlight into electrical energy. They are often used to provide electricity on spacecraft.

**Solar System** The Sun together with the eight planets (including Earth) and other bodies (such as dwarf planets, asteroids, and comets) that orbit it.

**solid-fuel rocket** A rocket in which the fuel and oxidant are both solids. Typically, solid-fuel rockets are simple metal tubes packed with a mixture of the propellants that are ignited to provide thrust. Solid-fuel rockets are less complex but more difficult to control than liquid-fuel rockets.

**sonic boom** The loud, thunder-like sound produced when an aircraft passes through the sound barrier.

**sound barrier** The abrupt increase in drag that occurs when an object approaches the speed of sound.

**Soviet** Of or from the USSR, a communist empire that existed from 1923 to 1990 and included present-day Russia, Ukraine, and Kazakhstan.

**supersonic** Traveling or capable of traveling faster than the speed of sound.

**telecommunications** Sending messages over a distance, usually involving electrical signals or electromagnetic waves.

**thrust** The force created by an engine that pushes an aircraft or spacecraft forward. Thrust is opposed by the drag created by moving through air.

**turbine** A machine made up of a set of blades mounted on a central shaft. A moving fluid, such as steam or air, makes the assembly rotate. Turbines are often used to drive generators.

**vacuum** A space that contains no matter.

**Vietnam War (1957–1975)** A conflict between communist North Vietnam (supported by the Soviet Union and China) and noncommunist South Vietnam (supported by the United States). U.S. soldiers were actively involved in the war from around 1965 to 1973, after which hostile public opinion in the United States forced their withdrawal. North Vietnam conquered the South in 1975.

**wingspan** The distance from one wing tip to the other.

**World War I (1914–1918)** A war fought mainly in Europe between the Central Powers—Germany, the Austro-Hungarian Empire (present-day Austria and Hungary), and the Ottoman Empire (now Turkey)—and the Allies: France, the British Empire, Russia, and the United States. The Allies eventually won the conflict, but millions of soldiers on both sides lost their lives.

**World War II (1939–1945)** The most destructive conflict in history, fought mainly in Europe, East Asia, and North Africa. The Axis powers (Germany, Austria, Japan, and Italy) were opposed by the Allies (Britain, the United States, France, and the USSR). Germany surrendered in April 1945, but Japan fought on until August, when atomic weapons dropped by U.S. aircraft destroyed the Japanese cities of Hiroshima and Nagasaki.

# FURTHER RESOURCES

## Books

*Daredevils of the Air: Thrilling Tales of Pioneer Aviators* by Karen E. Bledsoe. Greensboro: Avisson Press, 2003.

*Flight: 100 Years of Aviation* by Reg Grant. New York: Dorling Kindersley Publishers Ltd, 2010.

*The Outer Limits: The Future of Space Exploration* by Gary Miller. New York: Gareth Stevens Publishing, 2009.

*Test Pilots (The World's Most Dangerous Jobs)* by Antony Loveless. New York: Crabtree Publishing Company, 2009.

## Websites

*Discovery Channel: Exploring Space*
http://www.yourdiscovery.com/space/exploring/introduction/index.shtml

*NASA, Student website*
http://www.nasa.gov/audience/forstudents/index.html

*Centennial of Flight Commission*
http://www.centennialofflight.gov/user/kids.htm

*Howstuffworks: Jet Packs*
http://www.howstuffworks.com/transport/engines-equipment/jet-pack.htm

# INDEX